LEARN
BEFORE
YOU
LEAP

LEARN BEFORE YOU LEAP

101 CASE STUDIES FOR YOUTH PASTORS

KEVIN TURNER

ZONDERVAN®
.com

YOUTH
SPECIALTIES

ACADEMIC

ZONDERVAN.com/
AUTHORTRACKER
follow your favorite authors

ZONDERVAN

Learn Before You Leap
Copyright © 2012 by Kevin Turner

YS Youth Specialties is a trademark of YOUTHWORKS!, INCORPORATED and is registered
with the United States Patent and Trademark Office.

This title is also available as a Zondervan ebook.
Visit www.zondervan.com/ebooks.

Requests for information should be addressed to:

Zondervan, *Grand Rapids, Michigan* 49530

Library of Congress Cataloging-in-Publication Data

Turner, Kevin, 1962-
    Learn before you leap : 100 case studies for youth ministers / by Kevin Turner.
       p.   cm.
    ISBN 978-0-310-89029-4 (softcover)
    1. Church work with youth—Textbooks. I. Title.
  BV4447.T875 2012
  259'.23—dc23   2012015867

Cover design: Tammy Johnson
Cover photography: iStockphoto / Robert Kohlhuber
Interior design: David Conn

Printed in the United States of America

---

12 13 14 15 16 17 /DCI/ 23 22 21 20 19 18 17 16 15 14 13 12 11 10 9 8 7 6 5 4 3 2 1

CONTENTS

3. DEALING WITH DIFFICULT ISSUES

4. THE BIBLE, THEOLOGY, AND CHRISTIAN EDUCATION

5. RECREATION, RETREATS, AND ROAD TRIPS

6. WORSHIP, PRAYER, AND EVANGELISM

ACKNOWLEDGMENTS

Thank you . . .

To my parents, John and Sandy Turner, for your love, your examples, your encouragement, and your support in every endeavor of my life.

To First Presbyterian Church of Tacoma, Washington, for being a congregation that believed in youth ministry and preached the gospel in ways I could understand, believe in, and grow into. Thanks for developing my ministry skills through opportunities to serve with godly people like Chuck and Marie Hayden, Kirk Potter, Bob Gorham, and so many others. It was a pleasure and a joy to have served on your staff in many different roles over the years.

To Dr. Andy McQuitty, my first youth director and lifelong mentor. You were the first one to put your arm around me and ask if I'd ever considered "doing" youth ministry. I hadn't considered it then, but I can't imagine doing anything else now.

To Youth Specialties, for everything you've done to support youth workers and youth ministry. When I was a student, I played games from YS *Ideas* books. When I volunteered in youth ministry, it was a one-day YS seminar that helped me think about my own philosophy of ministry. When I entered full-time ministry, it was the National Youth Workers Convention and Mike Yaconelli who taught me how to feed my soul in a ministry context. When I began teaching, YS published the textbooks I used in class, and the YS academic support network became my community. Through the majority of my almost-50 years, Youth Specialties has been there at every step to help, inform, and inspire me. Since 1995 it has been a thrill to be involved on the NYWC staff along with Tic, Michelle, Marko, Mark, and so many others. Those relationships have been consistently life-giving, laughter-filled, and incredibly memorable.

To Colorado Christian University, whose administration, faculty, and students over the years have offered me a wonderful community in which to teach, learn, and grow. Dr. Larry Crabb and Dr. Sid Buzzell have modeled what Christ-centered academic service to the church looks like and have been great encouragers.

To Jay Howver, who read the initial proposal for this book and saw some promise, and to Doug Davidson, whose editing brought life and creativity that helped make a collection of case studies into a usable youth ministry resource.

To my incredible wife, Beth, who has been my fellow adventurer in the pilgrimage of life, my best friend, a selfless supporter, and a fellow parent of our two wonderful children, Paul and Madeleine—who are by far our best ministry work and our greatest joy.

> To all of you again I say,
> Thank you!

INTRODUCTION

Learn Before You Leap is a collection of one hundred one case studies designed to promote the growth and development of present and future youth workers. I believe that case studies are an underused tool that can allow youth workers to consider the kinds of real-life situations they'll face in their ministries. By allowing youth workers to think carefully about how they would respond to particular issues that arise in ministry and offering opportunities for them to discuss these situations with colleagues and mentors, this book will enable youth workers to leap more confidently into the situations they will encounter in their everyday work with youth.

In my own work as a teacher, I've utilized case studies in preparing young youth workers at the university level for twelve years. I've witnessed with my own eyes the increased engagement that students show when a case study is introduced. I've seen profound growth among students who have opportunities to discuss these potential ministry challenges with peers as well as with ministry veterans who have journeyed through the ups and downs of living out their calling. I can also testify to the power of case studies in my own growth and development as a minister, a professor, and a Christian. I'm convinced that one of the next logical steps in the maturing of the academic discipline of youth ministry is embracing the expanded use of case studies.

Since the 1980s I've been actively involved in local expressions of the National Network of Youth Ministry. I've been blessed beyond description by the fellowship, prayer, and relationships developed in those gatherings. As I look back, however, I wonder how much more I might have grown if our gatherings had included some intentional (yet informal) ongoing training with my fellow youth workers through case studies and conversation.

I believe today's developing youth workers need to wrestle with their own conclusions and convictions, rather than being spoon-fed pat answers. They want to be in relationships; they want to network; they want to discuss and brainstorm options with friends and mentors. They want a "heads up" about what they'll be facing in ministry so they can be prepared. They want to consider how they can apply what they've learned in real-life ministry settings. *Learn Before You Leap* offers them opportunities to do all that—and much more!

WHY CASE STUDIES?

Clyde F. Herreid of the University of Buffalo calls case studies "stories with a message." He continues, "They are not simply narratives for entertainment. They are stories to educate. Humans are story-telling animals. Consequently, the use of cases gives a teacher an immediate advantage; he has the attention of the audience."[1]

According to *The Oxford English Dictionary,* the term *case study* can be traced back to 1935, when the Harvard Business School began collecting real-life situations from business professionals. Those situations were then given to students who would think through possible strategies to address the opportunities and issues involved. In his 1948 book, *On Understanding Science,* chemist James Conant argued for the importance of using case studies in the natural and experimental sciences. Other fields of academic study—including the social sciences, law schools, and medicine—soon followed suit by including casework as part of their professional education. The use of case studies as a major focus in educating teachers was highlighted in a 1986 Carnegie report titled *A Nation Prepared: Teachers for the 21st Century.*

Organizations like The National Center for Case Study Teaching in Science at Buffalo University exist in order to promote the increased usage of case studies as either the core of entire courses or for single experiences in otherwise traditional lecture and lab courses. The Center's work over the past 15 years has found that "students exposed to the case study method have been extraordinarily excited and actively involved in their learning."[2]

British scientists Claire Davis and Elizabeth Wilcock have written

---

1. http://sciencecases.lib.buffalo.edu/CS/pdfs/What%20is%20a%20Case-XXVII-2.pdf

2. http://www.stem.project.mnscu.edu?index.asp?Type=B_dir&sec%7bE46FB54-E09F-4698-B3EC-FF232468EC%7d&DE=%7b27F7D47D-9BFC-44E7-9126-7499494ACA21%7d

about the use of case studies in scientific fields such as chemistry and engineering.[3] Based on their own experience, they cite more than 30 benefits stemming from the use of case studies, many of which apply directly to our context as youth workers. Davis and Wilcock argue that case studies can . . .

- bridge the gap between theory and practice;
- encourage active learning;
- develop key skills of problem-solving and communication;
- raise the level of critical thinking;
- build partnership and collegiality;
- prompt deeper diagnosis and meaning-making;
- provide a vehicle for examining multiple points of view;
- encourage attention to and self-consciousness about assumptions and conceptions;
- enhance listening and cooperative skills;
- help people monitor their own thinking and become aware of tension and ironies;
- encompass an enormous range of possibilities; and
- remind us that there may not always be one "right" answer after all!

When it comes to training for pastoral ministry, most seminaries and theological schools now make use of case studies as part of the field education portion of their curriculum. The American Association of Theological Schools has recognized the value of providing academically sound field education opportunities as part of the curriculum for future pastors. Case studies work hand-in-hand with field experience in allowing potential pastors to consider and reflect on the actual situations they will encounter in ministry. In their 1995 book *Experiencing Ministry Supervision,* William T. Pyle and Mary Alice Seals present case studies as their first suggestion for evaluating supervised ministry experience.[4] Reflecting on the importance of theological reflection as part of pastoral training, the authors suggest choosing "a ministry event in which you feel a pinch, an uncom-

---

3. Claire Davis and Elizabeth Wilcock, *Teaching Materials Using Case Studies* (Liverpool, United Kingdom: 2003, http://www.materials.ac.uk/guides/1-casestudics.pdf.
4. William T. Pyle and Mary Alice Seals, *Experiencing Ministry Supervision* (Nashville: Broadman and Holman, 1995), 101-103.

fortable feeling about your response. . . . The form is not as important as the fact that you are beginning with an event that raises questions."[5]

The ministry website www.xpastor.org is another strong advocate for the use of case studies in ministry training. Listen to how the site describes the benefits of case studies: "Case studies often leave the reader at the climax, forcing the reader to wrestle with the issues. . . . [Case studies] present a real-world example. It is as if they can be handled, touched, examined, and questioned."[6]

WHAT ABOUT YOUTH MINISTRY?

The field of youth ministry is already aware of the way case studies can be used to get students talking about real-life situations. In 1987, Jim Burns wrote *The Youth Worker's Book of Case Studies,* a collection of 60 studies designed to get kids talking. Ten years later Burns and Mark Simone released an updated and expanded version of that book called *Case Studies, Talk Sheets, and Discussion Starters.* The introduction states, "A case study goes deeper than an illustration by drawing us into the situation and asking us to face our own likely reactions even though we are not in reality involved. Learning occurs at a deeper level when we imagine how we would react or respond in a similar situation."[7] Citing the work of educator Edgar Dale, Burns underlines the value of case studies by noting that "when students are spoken or written to their retention level is only 5-10 percent, but when they are active participants in experiential learning the retention can be expanded to as much as 85 percent."[8]

In 2004, Steve L. Case authored *The Youth Worker's Big Book of Case Studies,* a collection of 180 case studies that promised to "get students talking" and "add sizzle, spice, and even a bit of controversy to your next meeting."[9] In my years of using case studies with middle school, high school, and college-aged students, I've found that they

---

5. Pyle and Seals, 113.

6. http://xpastor.org/seminar/welcome/case_studies.html

7. Jim Burns and Mark A. Simone, *Case Studies, Talk Sheets, and Discussion Starters* (Ventura, CA: Gospel Light, 1997), 12.

8. Burns, 11.

9. Steven L. Case, *The Youth Worker's Big Book of Case Studies* (Grand Rapids: Zondervan, 2004).

have done exactly what Case promises. But that raises a question: If we already know how effective case studies are in helping our students think through the real-life issues they are facing, why don't we make more intentional use of case studies in the training and continuing development of present and future youth workers?

As I've mentioned, I believe case studies can be a valuable part of the formal training that youth workers receive in a college or seminary program. But I also feel discussion of case studies can be a valuable way youth workers can benefit and grow from the wisdom and insights of their ministry colleagues. Paul Fleishman has identified the importance of "networking" both formally and informally as one of the keys to making our youth ministries more effective.[10] He notes that a key benefit of such networks is what he calls "sharpening," building on Proverbs 27:17—"As iron sharpens iron, so one person sharpens another." Fleishman quotes one youth worker veteran of 18 years as saying, "Why reinvent the wheel? If others are doing something successfully I want input from them." Another youth worker said he uses his network as a place to brainstorm ideas. Increased use of case studies makes the opportunities we have to network with other youth workers even more valuable.

Based on both the history and best practices of other disciplines, I believe the field of youth ministry could benefit greatly from the expanded use of case studies in both the formal training and ongoing development of youth workers. In addition to the theoretical argument, *Learn Before You Leap* provides 100 specific youth ministry case studies suitable for both formal and informal ministry education. At the end of the book you'll find a special chapter that offers guidance in developing your own case studies, so that you can stay up to date and relevant in the ever-changing world of youth ministry.

---

10. Paul Fleishman, "Where Can We Turn for Help in Youth Ministry?" *Reaching a Generation for Christ,* Mark Senter and Richard Dunn, eds. (Chicago: Moody Press, 1997), 547.

GETTING THE MOST FROM THIS BOOK

Different styles and genres of books need to be read in different ways—and this book is no exception. Whether you are using this book in a classroom setting, with a small group, or even on your own, the following "Do's and Don'ts" will help you maximize the value and impact of this book.

1. **Do feel free to skip around and choose the studies and topics that interest you most.** The famous "Do-Re-Mi" song from *The Sound of Music* suggests, "Let's start at the very beginning, a very good place to start." That's normally pretty good advice, but this book isn't designed to be read that way. *Learn Before You Leap* offers a multitude of topics, issues, and situations for your consideration. Not all of them will be equally applicable to your situation or ministry context, so be selective. Start with the case studies that most interest you and best fit your current needs. The studies are grouped together in thematic sections, but each individual study is designed to be read on its own. Even the introductory material is optional. In the introduction, I offer a justification for the use of case studies in both initial and lifelong youth ministry training. This material may be fascinating and helpful to you; if so—great. But if it's not, feel free to jump right into the case studies themselves.

2. **Don't rush.** As I've grown older, I've become more and more convinced that I'd be better off if I'd read less and reflected more. This book is designed for reflection. Your goal should not be to "finish it" but to use it to consider and prepare for the challenges that will crop up in your ministry, as you seek to share God's grace and truth with students. So go slow, take time to really think through the issues, and rehearse in your mind the specific words and actions you'd choose in each situation. Ponder the emotions that may be generated in you and in others involved in each case.

3. **Do write down your "answers."** Especially if you are reading the book on your own, you'll be tempted to answer the questions in your mind because it is so much faster and easier than writing answers down. But taking the time to record your responses helps ensure that you are giving careful attention to each question. Keep track of the date of your responses, and be sure to note any resources you found helpful in responding to the case. The advantages of putting your thoughts on paper are significant. Research has suggested that the process of writing can multiply retention of information as much as seven times.

4. **Don't skip questions.** One indication that you may be rushing through the material is the tendency to skip questions for which you don't have an immediate answer. The answer "I don't know" is entirely appropriate—as long as your next thought is "but I'll think it through, do some research, and formulate an answer." I wrote all these case studies, and I can't answer every question I've raised . . . but I'm working on them! The value of processing and discovering solutions and answers that you have wrestled through and now own is, after all, the real goal of using case studies.

5. **Do seek out ministry veterans with whom you can discuss these cases.** These studies are designed to start conversations about the practice of ministry. If you're new to youth ministry, seek out experienced youth workers with whom you can reflect on the issues raised by each case. It's almost impossible to overemphasize the value of relational support in maintaining long-term youth ministry viability. So use these case studies as a reason to expand and deepen your relational base and tap into others' expertise and life experience.

6. **Don't feel restricted by the specifics of the studies as written.** You can make the case studies more practical for your particular context by adjusting the descriptions to better match the students and adults with whom you work. Feel free to change details, alter names, and add additional questions that you can imagine one of your students asking. The key is usability, practi-

cality, and application—so take a stab at reworking the key concept or issue being presented to match your context.

7. **Do jot down additional questions.** You may find that other questions will come to your mind as you consider each situation and your perspectives on the issues it raises. Be sure to record those additional questions (and your answers) to maximize the value of the time you invest in thinking through these case studies.

8. **Do revisit case studies over time.** When you look back at studies you've considered previously, you'll have opportunities to see how your thoughts, convictions, and conclusions have become fine-tuned, adjusted, or confirmed. Looking back at your earlier answers can confirm your growth and development in the field of youth ministry and may give you more empathy for choices your younger youth ministry staff make that may now seem immature to you.

9. **Do use these case studies as an excuse to reach out to fellow youth workers.** There are a million reasons we are too busy to pick up the phone and connect with a fellow youth worker down the block or on the other side of the world. These case studies are much more interesting when discussed with others. There will be a slight temptation to "round up the usual suspects" and discuss these issues only with people whose thoughts and opinions you already know. Why not take a risk and dialogue with some youth workers from a slightly different tradition? Who knows—you might just learn something!

10. **Don't be afraid to write your own case studies.** Obviously, the one hundred case studies in this book can't address the near infinite number of situations you'll encounter as a youth worker. After spending some time on the cases in this book, you may well think of other situations you'd like to consider and discuss with other youth workers. So go ahead and try writing some studies of your own! At the end of the book you'll find a short appendix that offers some guidelines for writing effective case studies.

SO, YOU WANT TO BE A YOUTH WORKER...

HEARING THE CALL

You're sitting in your office preparing your talk for the Wednesday night youth meeting when you hear a knock on your door. Looking up, you see the coach of the freshman soccer team at the local high school. He's been a part of your congregation for some time, but you don't know him well. After you invite him in, he begins to talk about a student on his team who's been dealing with a lot of spiritual questions. Recently, the student made a profession of faith, and now the coach has been talking about Christ with the whole family. The coach tells you that nothing he's ever done has been as fulfilling as ministering to this family. "I guess I'm beginning to wonder," he says, "if God might be calling me to full-time youth ministry. But how can I know for sure?" What would you tell the young soccer coach sitting in front of you?

1. When did you first sense your own call to youth ministry? Where were you? Who were the key people involved?
2. How has your own calling to youth ministry been confirmed?
3. Have you ever gone through a time when you doubted your call to ministry? If so, what caused your doubts?
4. What errors have you observed in people trying to discern a call from God to vocational ministry?
5. What books or resources were helpful to you in discerning God's call to ministry?
6. Do you feel the calling to *youth* ministry is distinct from a call to ministry in general? Explain your answer.
7. How important are emotions and a desire to do ministry in sensing God's call?
8. Are all Christians called to ministry? If so, what is distinct about the call to professional or full-time ministry?
9. At what age can an individual begin to discern a call of God to vocational youth ministry? Or, to ask it another way, how would your response be similar or different if the person sensing God's call were a tenth-grader rather than a young adult?

SUSTAINABLE SCHEDULING

When the alarm blares in your ear, it takes all your energy to reach out and turn it off. Your achy body protests as you swing your feet onto the bedroom floor and head to the shower. It occurs to you that it's been a couple of weeks since your last day off; in fact, it's been *more* than a couple of weeks. The cycle of ministry seems endless; there are always student needs to address, leaders to train, talks to prepare, camps and retreats to plan, and administrative details to take care of, not to mention a seemingly endless series of staff meetings. It crosses your mind that the schedule you've established may not be sustainable. You realize you need to make a change soon or else you'll burn out entirely.

1. Have you ever felt "burned out" or overly fatigued in ministry? What steps did you take to bring yourself back to health?
2. What are your current practices in terms of a day off? How does your day off correspond to a Sabbath?
3. Someone once said, "Workaholism is a sin that the church applauds among its leaders." How do you respond to this quote?
4. What impact might ministry workaholism have in the following areas?

   - Personal walk with Jesus
   - Relationship with spouse
   - Modeling for students
   - Impact on other staff
   - Personal health
   - Parenting your own kids
   - Ministry longevity
   - Passion for ministry

5. How much annual vacation is appropriate for youth workers to receive?
6. Have you ever used "comp time" to overcome the impact of a busy ministry week?

7. What symptoms warn you that you are feeling burned out?
8. How many hours a week is appropriate for a youth minister to work? Explain.
9. Someone once said, "If the devil can't make you bad, he will make you busy." What is the problem with busyness in ministry?
10. Do you think ego and the "need to be needed" plays into a youth worker's inclination to overwork? Explain your answer.

THE MINISTRY PEDESTAL

As you say "Amen" to end the prayer, then say goodbye and watch the high school sophomore leave your office, you have a funny feeling in the pit of your stomach. You find yourself asking, "Did I handle that well?" Of course, students have asked you to pray for and with them before, but the wording of Jason's request stood out: "Can you pray for me?" he'd asked. "You see, my life is kind of messed up right now, and your prayers as a youth pastor are closer to God's ear than my prayers are." You find yourself wishing you'd questioned that assumption. You start to wonder if you've somehow allowed your students to think that you are connected to God in ways they could never be. Have you let them place you on a ministry pedestal?

1. Are some Christians more likely to have their prayers answered than others? Explain your answer.
2. When have you seen pastors or youth workers placed on a pedestal?
3. What are the dangers of allowing yourself to be thought of too highly?
4. What about the people you look up to? What are the dangers of placing unrealistic expectations on others?
5. Are there specific ways that you struggle with a feeling that you should appear to be more "spiritual" than you really are?
6. Why do you think some churches and ministries write unrealistic job descriptions that seem to assume that the right pastor or youth worker will solve all their problems? Why do you think people take on those jobs?
7. One ministry expert has written: "Pedestals become mutual conspiracies between pastors and people when pastors are treated as more spiritual by virtue of their office or calling."[11] Do you agree or disagree with this statement? Explain your answer.

---

11. "Number 8: What's the 8th deadly sin for church leaders today?" *Leadership Journal*, Spring 2001, 38-41.

8. What specific strategies can ministry professionals employ to avoid the tendency to cover up problems or intensify public religiosity to justify their positions?

9. Is it possible to walk in humility, repentance, forgiveness, and holiness while allowing others to place you on a ministry pedestal? Explain.

10. Is there any value to being placed on a pedestal as you lead others? If so, what is it?

DEALING WITH DISCOURAGEMENT

As you open the freezer door and grab the carton of butter-brickle ice cream, you reflect on the evening's board meeting. The agenda you'd been sent in advance had given no indication that this month's meeting was going to be devoted to beating down the youth pastor. As you think over the litany of accusations from parents, stark data about falling attendance at youth events, and even other pastoral staff misunderstanding your motives, it's not hard to figure out why you're feeling depressed and really, really tired. It crosses your mind that a job in your brother-in-law's plumbing warehouse might be a lot less stressful and maybe even more satisfying. But you're not quite ready to grab your laptop and begin writing your letter of resignation. At least not yet . . .

1. When was the last time you felt really discouraged in your ministry?
2. How important is other people's recognition of the value of your work to your sense of well-being in your ministry? Explain.
3. What is the relationship between "internal" and "external" call in discerning one's path in ministry? Does one overrule the other? Explain.
4. How do you remind yourself of the truth of your call when you get discouraged?
5. Who could you call for encouragement if you were feeling badly about your ministry situation?
6. What person has been most encouraging to you in your ministry? When and how was the last time you expressed your appreciation to that person?

MARRIED TO THE MINISTRY?

A church trustee pulls you aside after worship one Sunday. "You know, the wife of our previous youth pastor always attended every youth retreat as a chaperone, and she also led one of our middle school discipleship groups. I've noticed that your wife doesn't seem to attend many youth events . . ." You take a deep breath and remind yourself to count to ten before responding, but you know you'll have to count a lot higher than that for your heart to stop racing and your blood pressure to return to normal. It seems outrageous that the church would place expectations on your spouse based on your job description. As you slowly blow out your breath, you think through your response and say . . .

1. Have you ever had to deal with your church or minstry assuming your spouse will take on certain responsibilities in the youth ministry? If so, in what areas? How did you respond? How did your spouse respond?

2. What are reasonable expectations for a ministry spouse in the following areas?

   - Church attendance
   - Ministry participation
   - Small group leadership
   - Sunday school or Christian education
   - Vacation Bible School
   - Retreats or camps
   - Bible study groups

3. If you are employed by a congregation, how would church leadership respond if your spouse decided to get involved at another church down the street? How would you respond?

4. When you were hired for your latest ministry position, did you ask specifically about expectations for your spouse? If so, how did you frame the question? What was the response?

5. Does your ministry have expectations (whether explicit or implicit) for the spouses of its leaders in any of the following areas? If so, what are they?

   • Clothing (modesty or style)
   • Entertainment
   • Work/Career choices
   • Alcohol
   • Media choices
   • Hospitality/Entertaining
   • Child rearing and schooling

6. Do you think ministries generally treat ministry wives differently from ministry husbands? If so, how?

7. Respond to the following sentence: Due to the unique demands of professional ministry, the spouse of a youth worker must actively support the ministry if it is to be truly impactful and blessed by God.

"HELP, MY PARENT IS A YOUTH WORKER!"

As you drive home from the youth ministry conference, you keep rehashing the conversation that occurred around the lunch table that day. A few youth workers were talking about the unique challenges of raising their own kids while working in youth ministry. A few specific quotes stick in your mind . . .

"No one in the church ever disciplines my son because they're worried they will offend me or my spouse. He's becoming spoiled and acts like he's entitled to behave any way he chooses because I'm one of the pastors."

"I have the opposite problem—people seem to nitpick my kids, and speak up about any behavior they consider wrong or even childish. It's like my two daughters can't even be regular kids, just because I run the youth program. They are held to a higher standard than other kids, and it's not fair."

"I feel like our family lives in a fishbowl. Everybody at church thinks they know my kids well, and they feel free to provide suggestions, opinions, and insights. People come up and hug the kids at church— people they hardly even know. It's tough on them."

As you pull into the driveway, you can't help wondering about how your working with teenagers shapes the lives of your own children.

1. If you have kids of your own, which of these quotes most resonates with your experience? Which one represents the problem you believe to be the most prevalent experience among parents who do youth work?
2. What advice would you give to each of these youth workers?
3. Brainstorm the possible long-term impact of each of the above situations on the kids involved. What are the potential positives and negatives of each situation?
4. If you are the parent of teenage kids, what are your expectations about your children's involvement in your ministry?

GIFTED FOR YOUTH MINISTRY?

Sitting at the computer typing out the month's youth ministry finance report, you're happy to be distracted from this grueling task by an incoming email. And you're happy to see the note is from a former youth group member who is now in college studying to be a youth minister. She tells you that she has just taken a "spiritual gifts inventory" as part of a class, and the report indicated that her primary gifts were Helping, Giving, and Discernment. Her note closes with a question: "Do you think that mix of gifts would lead to a successful career in youth ministry?" How would you respond?

1. Do you know what your own spiritual gifts are? How did you determine them?
2. What is the ideal gift mix for a youth worker? Explain.
3. Do you use spiritual gift inventories in your ministry with students? Do you use them with high school students? How about middle-schoolers? Why or why not?
4. How important is the gift of "leadership" to success in youth ministry? Explain.
5. How do you explain the difference between spiritual gifts and natural talents?
6. How important is it to know the mix of spiritual gifts present among the other adult leaders (both paid and volunteer) in your youth ministry? Do you see any possible disadvantages to knowing this information?
7. Do you believe there are other spiritual gifts in addition to those specifically listed in the New Testament? For example, would you consider worship leading, small group facilitation, or the ability to build a great ministry website to be spiritual gifts? Why or why not?
8. Do spiritual gifts require training to be used most effectively? Explain.

9. What is the relationship between your ministry's needs and your own spiritual gifts? Is it ever right to say no to a legitimate need because it is "not my gift"? Explain.

10. What would you say to a Christian student who tells you she doesn't have a spiritual gift?

BOUNDARIES AND ACCESSIBILITY

Just as the first forkful of hot, delicious spaghetti reaches your lips, the jarring melody of your ringtone blares at you from your pocket. Under the withering stare of your spouse (who's been planning this special birthday dinner all week), you pick up the phone to see who is interrupting your dinner hour. It is, of course, one of the kids from your youth group—one who's really been struggling over the past few weeks. As you excuse yourself from the table to take the call ("It will only be a minute," you say), you think back over the past week and the midnight phone call from a concerned parent, the early morning call from a staff member, and the heated argument with your spouse concerning your availability to students seemingly at all hours of the day and night. You begin to wonder whether you need to set some different boundaries about your own availability.

1. Do you have a current policy about your availability to students by phone? What are the rules? Are you satisfied with the existing policy? Why or why not?
2. How does your personal availability compare with the availability of others on the staff of your church or ministry?
3. Respond to the following statement: If you are available to students 24 hours a day, then they never will learn to depend on God and walk by faith.
4. Do you think wanting to be available to students at all times signifies a healthy desire to "be there" for students or is it a sign of a "messiah complex"? Explain your answer.
5. What boundaries do you have in place regarding students dropping by your home? How about your office?
6. When you go on vacation, do you leave a "number where you can be reached"? Why or why not?
7. Are there any kinds of "emergencies" that would necessitate a phone call interrupting your family vacation? What would it be?

8. Have you ever taken a "Sabbath" from your cell phone? Why or why not? Have you ever challenged your students to take a technology Sabbath? Why or why not?
9. Are you personally accessible to students through Facebook, Twitter, IM, email, or other social networking options? Why or why not?

LONGEVITY IN MINISTRY

You stand up and cheer loudly as the conference leader reads the list of youth ministry veterans who've been doing professional youth work for more than twenty years, including at least ten years in their current position. A tear forms in the corner of your eye as you reflect on the hurdles these faithful servants have overcome. Such longevity in ministry is what you strive for, in part because you are very aware of the negative impact that a church or ministry experiences when its staffing is unstable or frequently in transition. As you gather your belongings to depart from the meeting, you recommit in your heart to make longevity in ministry a focused priority. But what can you do to make that commitment a reality?

1. What are some of the positive impacts of ministry longevity on the following areas?

    - For students
    - For families
    - For the church or ministry organization
    - For the youth worker

2. What are some of the potential pitfalls of remaining in a particular ministry location for a long time?
3. What is the optimum length of ministry in a particular location or position? Does it vary depending on the individual or the ministry setting? Explain your answer.
4. What are the major roadblocks that hinder ministry longevity both in a single location and over a whole career?
5. Respond to this thought: If you have served in four different locations in a 20-year ministry career, you don't have 20 years of experience but five years of experience repeated four times.
6. Is longevity the key factor in calculating ministry success? Why or why not?

7. Ministry has been defined as "the glory of the grind." How do you find "glory" in the everyday grind of your work?

8. What specific elements have you built into your schedule to help promote ministry longevity?

9. Does your church or ministry offer staff members a sabbatical as a tool to promote long-term ministries? What are strengths and weaknesses of youth ministry sabbaticals?

10. True or false: Many people leave the ministry when what they really need is a vacation. Explain your answer.

11. What are some things churches and ministry organizations could do that would promote ministry longevity? Why don't more churches and ministry organizations practice these ideals?

12. When Dwight L. Moody was asked how he had sustained his ministry for so long, he replied, "I have never lost the wonder." What do you think he meant? In what ways is "wonder" important in sustaining long-term ministry?

TWEEN YEAR

"Please, you just *have* to speak with Pat." The mother of a senior in your ministry is standing before you, an anguished look on her face. "Pat has this crazy idea that he needs to take a 'tween year' between high school graduation and the start of college. The idea is to travel, work a bit, take some time away from school, and just 'grow up' before going on to the university. We are absolutely against this wild idea. To us, it just sounds like an excuse to not grow up and accept responsibilities. It will be expensive, and we're afraid Pat may not decide to go on to college at all. Plus, it seems foolish not to take advantage of the scholarships he's been offered and go to school with the others in his graduating class. If you can't convince me of the value of a 'tween year experience,' we're going to say no and place a deposit for him to begin college in the fall." What would you say to this parent about the strengths and weaknesses of a "tween" year?

STING OPERATION

"So I asked if you'd meet me for lunch because I have a bit of an unusual request." Officer Sharpe was a respected member of the local police force and had been a member of your congregation for years—but he'd never shown much interest in the youth ministry before. "I'm wondering if you and your students might help us with a series of sting operations at local convenience stores in your area. There have been reports of alcohol and tobacco being sold to minors. We'd like you to drive your students to a few local stores we are concerned about and have them go in and try to buy alcohol or cigarettes with some marked bills that we would supply. If they're questioned about their age, the students should never lie, but simply leave and fill out a favorable report. But if a sale is made, you would bundle the receipt, change, and contraband, and then fill out an incident report so we can take appropriate action. We would, of course, provide the necessary forms to get parental permission for any kids involved. It would be like a service project helping promote lawfulness and order in your community. What do you think?"[12]

1. Would you agree to have students participate in this effort? Why or why not?
2. What additional questions would you need to have answered?
3. Are there particular lessons you'd hope your students would learn from this experience?
4. What do you think parents' responses would be to your ministry's participation in this sting operation?

---

12. When I shared this case study with college students in a recent youth ministry class, some laughed and said the situation sounded unlikely. But like all the studies in this book, this case is based directly on real experience. When I was a youth pastor at a church in the northwest, our ministry supplied students for exactly this kind of sting operation for several years. Although I am not certain how I'd respond to the same request today, our students found the experience fascinating. I understand the city still uses students from local youth ministries in such operations.

TIME TO MOVE ON?

As you shuffle along kicking the fallen leaves, you feel your apprehensiveness growing. Things have not been going particularly well in your ministry lately. Most days you find yourself feeling worn out before you even get to the office in the mornings. You begin to imagine how nice it might be to get a fresh start in another city, and you wonder if the ministry could benefit from different leadership. You begin to wonder: What are the signs that God is calling you to another ministry location—or even calling you to leave vocational ministry entirely?

1. How does one know when the time is right to leave a particular ministry?
2. When is the best time to leave a ministry position? When things are going well and the ministry is strong? When momentum is low and change seems needed? Explain your answer.
3. Whose advice would you seek if you were considering a ministry transition? Why?
4. What questions need to be answered before deciding on a ministry move?
5. Name five key principles for leaving a ministry well.
6. Ideally, how much time should elapse between when you decide to leave a ministry and when you actually depart?
7. How can you determine when God is calling you to a new ministry as opposed to simply feeling tempted to leave because you are feeling bored or frustrated?
8. Is there a minimum amount of time that you should spend in any given ministry position before even considering a move? Explain.
9. What information could you provide that would be essential or helpful to the person who takes over your current position?
10. What are the most important things that need to be communicated to students and their parents when a youth leader leaves? Explain.

11. Ideally, what steps should a church or ministry take if it decides a youth worker needs to be replaced involuntarily?

12. Which of the following do you currently do? Why?

- Keep an updated résumé
- Check current ministry job openings
- Have a pre-written letter of resignation
- Have an emergency fund in case of unexpected job loss

PART OF THE PROBLEM?

Climbing into your car after Sunday worship, you see the dad of one of your youth approaching you with a bemused expression on his face. "Sorry to bother you as you're headed home, but I have a couple of questions I hope you can help me with. I was with my brother-in-law the other night and he insisted that I watch a film called *Divided*.[13] Have you ever heard of it?" Before you have a chance to answer he continues, "Well, it's a film about all the problems with youth ministry. My brother-in-law says it really impacted him; in fact, after watching it he pulled his own kids out of the youth ministry program at his church. The film claims that youth ministry is a totally modern invention that's contrary to Scripture. He says youth ministries do more harm than good because they isolate youth from the larger church in a way that is unbiblical, and it ends up creating a pandemic of teenagers who drop out of church after they graduate high school and leave the youth programs. There were lots of interviews, and the argument didn't really feel right, but I didn't know how to respond. I am going to see my brother-in-law again next week, and he wants to talk about my responses to the film. Can you help me answer his concerns?"

1. What would you say to this parent?
2. Have you ever personally encountered any "anti-youth ministry" sentiment?
3. How would you answer the specific charges levied against youth ministry in the video?
4. Do you feel any of the concerns in the film have merit? If so, how might you adjust your ministry practices to account for them?

---

13. For more information on the film and its critique of current youth ministry practices, see www.dividedthemovie.com.

2

MUSIC, MEDIA, AND THE MESSAGE

MUSIC MATTERS

The senior pastor walks through the gym late Friday night to grab some sermon notes she'd left in the office. You're in the middle of a high school event with some rather loud music playing. A few of the girls are dancing; most of the guys are shooting hoops. The pastor smiles and waves to you on the way out. On Monday morning, she casually asks what kind of music you were playing that night.

1. What role(s) does music play in your ministry? Reflect on the extent to which you use music in each of these ways:

   - As background music
   - To set a mood
   - To illustrate talks or teaching
   - For student worship
   - To prompt discussions
   - For evangelism

   - To invite student participation in worship (youth choir, bells, orchestra, etc.)
   - For social times
   - Other

   _____

2. Do you find the terms *Christian* and *secular* helpful in describing music? Why or why not?

3. Do you think all music at ministry-sponsored events should be performed by Christian artists? Why or why not?

4. What Christian artists or bands would you recommend for use at youth events? What "secular" artists would you recommend?

5. What about your own personal music preferences? Is most of your music Christian? Secular? A mix? What artists and bands make up your playlist?

6. Does the focus or target audience of an event influence your decision on music use? How about the age of the students (middle school vs. high school)?

"AUTHORIZED" MUSIC

You're sitting at your desk on a Monday morning trying to clear your head with a cup of coffee when the telephone rings. You answer it to hear the voice of an angry mom whose son is an active middle school student in your ministry. She's calling to complain about Zach, a college-aged volunteer in your ministry. While Zach was driving a group of middle-schoolers home after a weekend event, he played a CD on the car stereo that had a parent advisory label on the cover. Graphic lyrics were blasting through the car's sound system all the way home. "That's not what I expect when I send my 13-year-old on a church retreat!" she tells you. "What are you going to do about this?"

1. What will you say to this parent?
2. Are you concerned about the personal listening habits of staff and adult volunteers in your ministry?
3. What, if anything, will you say to Zach about the music he played while driving the students home?
4. Does your ministry have a policy about the music staff and volunteers will listen to in the presence of students? If so, what is the policy? Do all staff and volunteers know the policy?
5. Does your policy change if the students being driven home are high school juniors and seniors rather than middle-schoolers? Why or why not?
6. Do students know your ministry position regarding the music staff listens to in their presence? How and when do you communicate it to them?

TEACHING ABOUT MEDIA

"Next month we'll begin our series on Movies, Music, and Media." These words send a small shiver down your spine even as they come from your mouth. You realize the way television, film, music, and other popular media shape the lives of your young people, and you want to help kids develop a discerning approach to the input that comes at them from all directions. But you also realize the potential for controversy and different convictions within your ministry and the church at large. One of the first steps is to select resources to support your efforts, beginning first with background information for you and your staff and then moving on to tools you can share with your students. This leads you to reflect on several important questions . . .

1. What books and other resources do you have at this time to help you understand media? How up-to-date and useful are these materials? If you were to purchase new resources, in what areas would you want to focus?
2. What authors, speakers, and other experts do you most trust? What have they done to earn your trust?
3. How often should effective youth ministries teach about media? Why?
4. In a multi-week series, what key ideas, Scriptures, and application steps would you want to cover with your students?
5. Are there any particular Bible passages you will be sure *NOT* to use because you have seen them misused in the past?
6. If students ask (and they probably will!), how will you answer the following questions about your own media choices?

   • What bands or recording artists do you listen to most often? Why?
   • What's your favorite movie? Why?
   • What TV shows do you watch frequently?
   • How do you evaluate whether to see a movie or purchase a recording?

- Do you attend R-rated movies? Why or why not?

7. What websites would you recommend to your students to help them evaluate media choices?

GARBAGE IN, GARBAGE OUT

After hearing that you'll be teaching a series on Christian perspectives on media, a middle school parent emails you suggesting that the old computer-programming slogan "Garbage In, Garbage Out" would make a great theme for such a series. She adds that if you like the theme and decide to use it for your series, she'd be willing to have T-shirts professionally made for all the kids with the phrase printed across the front. What do you think of the theme? Does it resonate with your approach to media? Will you take this parent up on her offer to buy the shirts? Why or why not?

"PLEASE DON'T TELL MY PARENTS!"

You are preparing to take a group of ninth-graders on their fall retreat. As you walk toward the back of the bus to move a suitcase from the aisle, you notice two guys sitting in the back of the bus listening to an iPod and laughing. Just making conversation, you ask what they're listening to. Their faces go deadly white at first, then turn bright pink with embarrassment. It turns out they're listening to a comedian whose material is very profane and sexually explicit. Both students happen to be children of members of the church staff. They beg you not to tell their parents what they were listening to. "If my dad finds out about this," one guy laments, "he's not gonna let me download anything else until I'm 30!"

1. What's your initial response to these students?
2. What follow up, if any, will you require with them?
3. Do you feel you need to mention this to their parents? Why or why not?
4. Does the fact that the parents of these guys are on the church staff affect the way you deal with this situation? Why or why not?
5. How much oversight do you believe parents should have over a ninth-grader's listening habits?
6. What biblical passages or principles inform your thinking about this situation?
7. Would your response to the situation change if the students were 17-year-old seniors? What if they were sixth-graders?
8. In general how do you balance students' right to privacy versus parents' right to know what their children are doing?
9. Given this situation, reflect on the relative importance of the following factors:

    • Student privacy
    • Negative impact of sexually explicit media
    • Staff member loyalty

- Impressionability of students
- Parent's right to know
- Trust between youth worker and students
- Trust between youth worker and parents
- Youth leader–student confidentiality

CONNECTED OR DISCONNECTED?

The miles are rolling by as you drive the ministry van with eleven students to a wonderful week at a camp in a neighboring state. Your mind's been filled with the details of your upcoming responsibilities, until it strikes you that the students are completely silent. You'd steeled yourself for endless verses of "99 Bottles of Pop on the Wall," but it's so quiet you could hear a pin drop. You sneak a glance over your shoulder, expecting you'll find the students sleeping. But everyone is awake, they're just not communicating—at least not with one another. Every single kid is plugged into a set of headphones. Most are listening to iPods (while simultaneously texting on their phones), a few others are playing video games on their phones or a gaming device, and one kid is watching the latest Will Ferrell movie on his iPad. You'd hoped the drive would provide a time for students to get to know one another and build community, but every kid is in his or her own digital world. How do you respond?

1. Are personal listening devices a barrier to building community in youth ministry? Explain your answer.
2. Do you have any rules about the use of personal music players during travel?
3. Does the integration of tasks (like phones that play music) make rules harder to enforce?
4. Brainstorm some ideas about how to make travel engaging for today's students.
5. Have you encountered students using personal video devices to watch movies or TV shows while on trips? How has this positively or negatively impacted student interaction?
6. How do you think parents of students in your ministry would respond if you limited access to cell phones during ministry trips?
7. Is it reasonable to institute a "no headphone" period during travel to promote student communication? What do you think initial student response to such a policy would be?

8. What policies do you have about the use of the music systems in church van or buses while traveling on ministry trips?
9. Is Jesus' teaching on fasting applicable to music and media? Why or why not?

FALL RETREAT LULLABY

The clock reads 12:04 a.m. as you and a group of ninth-graders pour into the dorm room at the retreat center. The first day of the fall retreat went well—the program was interesting; the teaching was impactful; even the food was good! You smile as you encourage students to streamline their bedtime rituals so you can all get some sleep. As you turn around to set up your own sleeping bag, you notice a couple of students arranging their iPods right beside their pillows. When you remind them that it's time for shut-eye not music, several youth (and one adult leader) immediately protest that they can't possibly fall asleep without listening to music. One guy playfully adds, "Plus, have you ever heard how Eric snores!" You don't want kids up all night listening to music, but you don't want to disrupt a good night's rest and ruin the next day's events. What do you do?

MOVIE MADNESS!

You haven't even settled into your office chair yet on a summer Monday morning when the phone rings. You answer to hear the voice of a very angry parent. It seems that after the youth meeting last night, a large group of students and a few members of the ministry staff headed over to the nearby home of a student to watch a movie. This parent was shocked to learn that the movie they'd shown carried an "R" rating, which violated their family's standards for their ninth-grade daughter. "When she called to ask permission, she told me she didn't know what movie they were going to show, but that a couple of the staff would be there, so I figured it was fine. I didn't expect your ministry would be endorsing such trash!" You explain that the movie wasn't a ministry-sponsored event, but that does little to satisfy her. And you learn later that the senior pastor's eighth-grade son was also in attendance, so you have a feeling this won't be the only conversation you'll be having about this event! What will you say to this parent and others who call?

1. Does attendance by youth ministry staff make a gathering a youth ministry event? Why or why not? What will you say to the youth ministry staff in attendance?
2. Will you take a proactive approach to avoid this situation in the future? If so, how?
3. What would you have said to the parent on the phone if your youth staff had *not* been present—if it were just a group of students who'd gathered to watch a movie after youth group?
4. Will you say anything to the student who hosted and selected the movie? To the parents of that student? To the whole youth group?

"LIKE" MY PHOTO?

The church administrative assistant who helps facilitate the youth ministry program walks into your office with a chagrined look on her face. "Have you seen the Facebook page that several students set up after last weekend's retreat? Apparently, they wanted a place to connect and share pictures—and are they ever sharing pictures! I'm sure the retreat had some great spiritual content, but the pictures they're posting have no context and seem a bit bizarre and weird. I've already had three calls from concerned parents who want photos of their children removed from the site, and another call from a board member who wants an explanation of what's going on in two of the pictures. I told them you'd call them back." As you consider a morning full of tense phone conversations, you reflect on a number of issues.

1. Do you make use of Facebook in your ministry? Why or why not? If so, how?
2. Do you have a personal Facebook page? If so, what are your policies regarding "friending" your students?
3. Have you had to deal with inappropriate Facebook postings in the past? How did you handle the situation?
4. What are the most important guidelines that every student in your ministry should know about using Facebook and other social media well?
5. With the realities of cell phone cameras and the Internet, every youth ministry gathering is potentially a public event. How does this shape your ministry?
6. How will you respond to the concerned people you are about to call?

MOVIES ON "MY TIME"

As you leave the corner theater of the local multiplex, you notice a couple of ministry staff members buying popcorn in the lobby. When you casually ask what they're planning to see, they excitedly and without embarrassment tell you the name of the film. It's a blockbuster horror film that's been getting a lot of attention, at least in part because of its graphic sexuality, gratuitous violence, and crude humor. As you turn to leave, you find yourself hoping that none of your students (or their parents) see your staff members entering the theater or hear them talking about the film afterward. Would you speak to your staff at the theater? Later? What would you say to them? How would you respond if they said it's no one's business what movies they watch on their own time, as long as students aren't involved?

MOVIE CLIPS AND MINISTRY

As you prepare for your Wednesday night youth talk, you search your brain for a great illustration on the theme of "sacrifice." You suddenly recall a powerful scene from *Saving Private Ryan* that would be perfect for your point, but at the very same time you also recall the controversy from the last time you used a clip from an "R" rated movie. Several parents felt like your use of the clip confused students and was taken as the church's endorsement of a movie that included foul language, sexual situations, drug use, and violence. For a while the whole episode made you avoid using any film clips at all for teaching. But this scene seems perfect. Do you use the clip? And if you do, how do you explain your rationale to parents?

1. Does your use of a movie clip imply approval of the movie? Why or why not?
2. What standards do you use in selecting clips in relationship to the following areas:

    - Ratings
    - Subject material
    - Language
    - Violence

3. Does the lifestyle of the movie star in a clip influence your willingness to use the clip? Why or why not?
4. Are your standards for clip usage different for middle school students as opposed to those in high school? If so, how?
5. How do you respond to parents whose standards about video content are much more restrictive than your own?
6. Have you ever used a movie clip that bombed? Have you ever used a clip that was exceptional in its impact on students? What made the difference? What is the ideal length of a clip? Why?
7. What standards do you have regarding ministry use of nonrated videos (such as You-Tube clips)?

MUSIC "PIRATING"

The youth meeting ended a while ago, and most of the students have already left. As you chat with a few lingering parents, you notice two high school girls hovering around your laptop. Earlier in the evening you'd used your computer to play a couple of songs to illustrate the biblical content of your message. As you walk over, you see that the students have connected a USB cord to the computer and are downloading the song you'd used to an MP3 player. They don't seem embarrassed; in fact, they smile and tell you how much the song impacted them. You feel pleased and a little flattered—until the words *copyright infringement* pop into your mind. How do you handle the situation?

1. Would you permit the students to continue downloading the song? Why or why not?
2. How do you understand the "fair use" regulations regarding ministry use of copyrighted music in teaching and worship?
3. Respond to this statement: Piracy of music is so widespread among youth today that individual resistance is futile.
4. How consistent is your ministry in its adherence to copyright regulations? For example, consider the showing of videos at public events, photocopying sheet music for the praise band, or making unauthorized copies of curriculum.
5. How would you respond if the students protested: "These artists make so much money, they don't need any more cash. After all, you paid for the songs, didn't you? Aren't we just sharing resources?"

COPYRIGHT CONCERNS

While previewing a DVD for a middle school lock-in, you notice for the first time the wording of the FBI warning that precedes every feature presentation. Most of the warning doesn't apply to you in any way, but the phrase "the public display of this copyrighted film is prohibited and punishable by law" seems to be exactly what you are about to do. Is showing a DVD to kids at a ministry lock-in a violation of copyright law? If you are not sure, how could you find out?

VIDEO GAMES

You've just hosted about 15 seventh-grade guys for a midweek evening of video-gaming. As you turn off the power on the church's flat screen TV, you celebrate that the event drew a few guys you'd never seen at the church before. But later that night as you drive home, you find yourself wondering—and not for the first time—about the validity of gaming as a youth ministry strategy. Sure, the guys had a blast. But there are, of course, the costs and the seemingly endless need to upgrade to newer, faster systems with better graphics. Then there is the question of what games are "appropriate" for a ministry context. And, of course, the time spent playing the games isn't exactly what one would call "quality relationship-building time." As you lie in bed that night, you find yourself continuing to weigh the merits of using video games in the youth room.

1. Does your ministry own—or have access to—a gaming system? If so, how have you used gaming in your ministry?
2. Do you game on your personal time? Why or why not? If you play, what games are your favorites?
3. Do you game regularly with students? What games do you play? Why?
4. In your opinion what is a "reasonable" amount of time for a student to spend gaming over the course of a week? Explain your answer.
5. What would you say to a parent who stated, "Gaming is a complete waste of time. Instead of playing games with students, we should be warning them about the addictive nature of these games"?
6. Do you have a biblical/theological perspective on gaming? Have you ever taught about it? What Scriptures speak to this issue?
7. How concerned are you about videogame violence and "first-person shooter games"? Do you play these games personally? Do you use them in ministry? Why?
8. What is your opinion about the rating system for games? Do you follow it? Why?

RATED M FOR MATURE?

The flyer was handed to you by a youth worker from the megachurch across town: "Come be a part of our huge evangelism outreach event! We've connected our gaming systems to the church's big-screen DPUs and we're doing a Halo 3 tournament. After a few hours of gaming, we'll have pizza and then an evangelist who is going to build off the elements of the game to present the gospel. Can we expect you and your students?" How would you respond to this invitation? What reasons would you give for your decision?

5. In general, what counseling issues do you feel comfortable handling yourself? What issues are you completely unprepared to deal with?

6. Have you ever referred a student to a counseling specialist? If not, whom could you contact to find out how to handle counseling referrals responsibly?

COUNSELING QUESTIONS

The knock on your office door was so gentle you barely heard it. When you open the door, you see Shelly, a junior from your youth group. "Can I talk to you?" she asks, with a very tentative look on her face. "I have some stuff going on that I hope you can help me with." The conversation begins with a few general comments about friends at school but quickly turns more serious and personal. She tells you she's feeling great pressure about grades, she's worried about her college choices, and has just broken up with her long-time boyfriend. She looks very thin, and it crosses your mind that she might be struggling with an eating disorder. "I don't know," she says. "I just feel like I'm falling apart these days." As you focus on what she's telling you, your mind is bombarded with questions not only about how you can support Shelly, but about the whole process of counseling and your role in helping hurting students.

1. Is your office a safe place to meet with students? What is one thing you could do to make your office "safer" for counseling sessions? Is there another place that would be more appropriate for such meetings?

2. Do you ever counsel students of the same gender alone? Why or why not? Would you ever counsel a student of the opposite gender alone? Under what circumstances?

3. What policies have you established to protect yourself from compromising situations as well as from false accusations of improper student interaction?

4. According to a 1994 study by the Southern Baptist Convention, 71 percent of ministers who became involved in an adulterous affair reported that the affair started through counseling sessions.[14] What elements of accountability do you practice in your counseling? In light of the above research, do you need to add more?

---

14. Randolph K. Sanders, ed., *Christian Counseling Ethics* (Downers Grove, IL: Inter-Varsity, 1997), 84.

STRUGGLING WITH DIVORCE

"My parents are getting a divorce." As the ninth-grade guy standing before you begins to weep, the enormity of his statement begins to sink in. You know that life will never be the same for him and his family; you also know that how you respond and follow up with this student will make a big difference in the healing process. You pause and take a deep breath, and then begin to speak . . .

1. What are the first words that you would say in response to this news? What do you most want this student to hear in this situation?
2. How has your own life been touched by divorce? What emotions does the word conjure up within you? Are there personal feelings you need to deal with more fully before you can be truly helpful to youth whose lives are affected by divorce? Explain your answer.
3. List all the emotions you might expect to see expressed by students whose families are experiencing divorce. Think about how you will respond to students experiencing each of these emotions.
4. Outline a plan for long-term follow-up with a student whose family is undergoing a divorce.
5. Many young people experience a great deal of personal guilt about their parents' divorce. How will you specifically address the possible guilt feelings?
6. Many children struggle to forgive their parents for the pain the parents' divorce has caused. What Scripture and thoughts will you share with a student regarding forgiveness?
7. What resources would you give to students to help them deal with and understand the divorce process?
8. What advice would you give to parents who want to minimize the negative impact of a divorce on their child?
9. In what situations would you refer a student going through a divorce to a professional counselor?

ENCOUNTERING SUICIDE

As you bend over to grab a dirty paper cup from the floor after the Wednesday night meeting, your eyes settle on a torn sheet of notebook paper. Standing up to read the crudely printed note, you feel your heart begin to sink: "I hate my life. I have no friends, and I hate this ministry. No one cares or even talks to me. I wonder if life is worth living or if death might be the best end to all my pain." As you sink into a nearby chair, your mind begins to race as you ponder what you should do next . . .

1. What are your first actions if you suspect a student might be contemplating suicide?
2. To whom would you refer a suicidal student? How would you handle the referral?
3. Have you ever taught on the topic of suicide? How often? What resources have you used in your teaching?
4. Have you ever shared with staff any resources for dealing with suicide? Why or why not?[15]
5. H. Norman Wright has listed twenty different warning signs of adolescent suicide.[16] What signs are you aware of that might indicate that a youth is contemplating suicide?
6. On a scale of 1 to 10, how prepared do you feel to respond to a student who shares that he or she is considering suicide? If you feel unprepared, how can you get the information or training you need?

---

15. One excellent Web-based resource on this topic can be found at www.suicidepreventionlifeline.org.
16. H. Normal Wright, *Crisis Counseling: What to Do and Say in the First 72 Hours* (Ventura, CA: Regal Books, 1993), 139.

3

DEALING WITH
DIFFICULT ISSUES

COMPLETELY CONFIDENTIAL

At the conclusion of a small-group Bible study, a freshman guy comes up to you and says: "I have a very serious issue I need to talk to you about. But I need you to promise that you'll keep it absolutely confidential. You can't tell *anyone*." How would you respond?

"I THINK I'M PREGNANT"

Ashley, a high school junior, has been a part of your youth ministry for about a year. Several months ago, her boyfriend David began attending Sunday night meetings with her. Both of them are well liked by both students and staff. Late on a Thursday afternoon, they poke their heads into your office and ask if they can talk with you. They sit down and, after a few minutes of small talk about the upcoming retreat, they blurt out the real reason they sought you out. They have been sexually active recently, and they now suspect Ashley may be pregnant. Their eyes speak volumes about the anguish and anxiety they're both experiencing. What are the first words that will come out of your mouth?

1. Where would you suggest Ashley go to receive medical care and confirmation of the pregnancy?
2. How and when would you counsel them to tell their parents and families? What role, if any, will you play in that process? Explain your answer.
3. How and when will this information be shared with the youth staff? With other students? With the wider congregation?
4. If the possibility of an abortion is raised, how will you respond?
5. If they ask about the possibility of adoption, what will you say? To whom will you refer them?
6. Many counseling experts recommend never asking a person in crisis, "What are you going to do?" because the question can feel overwhelming. Do you agree or disagree with this advice? Why?
7. What specific counsel will you provide to Ashley? What about David? What issues might he be dealing with?
8. What sort of practical support will you and your ministry or congregation provide for David and Ashley? Check all that apply—and explain your reasons.

    _____ Baby shower
    _____ Babysitting help
    _____ Financial assistance

_____ Parenting classes

_____ Parenting mentors

_____ Educational support

_____ Professional counseling

_____ Adoption services

_____ Corporate prayer

9. How will you follow up with Ashley and David if medical tests find that Ashley is not pregnant?

CUTTING AND SELF-INJURY

You'd noticed that Monica always wore long sleeves no matter how hot the weather was—and yesterday you found out why. Monica's mom came in and tearfully told you that her precious 15-year-old daughter had been cutting herself for the past 18 months. You shake your head in utter disbelief. Self-injuring has become an epidemic among youth today, with students as young as middle school actively involved. One British medical journal estimates that 13 percent of 15- and 16-year-olds intentionally injure themselves.[17] As you mentally crunch the number of students you minister to regularly, you realize it's very unlikely that Monica is the only "cutter" in your group. You know you need to help Monica get the support she needs, but you also feel an immediate need to teach on the subject at an upcoming ministry gathering. As you head to your desk to begin work on the presentation a number of questions crowd to the forefront of your thinking.

1. What signs should parents, teachers, and youth workers look for that may indicate self-injurious cutting? Is there a profile of a "typical" cutter?

2. What would you say to a teenage cutter? What would you say to his or her parents?

3. Experts suggest forming a team to help a cutting student. Who would you seek out to be a part of such a team?

4. What resources will you provide to staff and parents to help them understand the issues surrounding self-injury?

5. Self-injury is often a coping mechanism that teenagers use to release strong emotions. What practical suggestions could you give to help students deal with overwhelming emotions?

6. List a series of "do's and don'ts" for students, parents, and youth workers addressing the issue of cutting with a student.

7. Who in your community (professional counselor) do you trust enough to refer a self-injurious student?

17. www.teenhelp/teen-health/cutting-stats-treatment.html

SCHOOL SUCCESS AND STRUGGLES

"I am in serious trouble in Biology this semester. I'm getting a D right now, and Mr. Andrews says we haven't even got to the tough stuff yet!"

"I'm going to get grounded for my grades too," Susan chimed in, as several other students nodded. "My parents say I need to study harder, or they won't let me do any outside activities—including youth meetings and the mission trip!"

"I wish I had your problem," Hilary protested, "I'm taking three AP classes, but my parents throw a fit if I don't get a 4.0 every semester. If I even get a B on a test, I feel like a total failure!"

Your own memories of high school classes feel much less intense than the emotions expressed by your students. You find yourself asking, "How can I help students who are dealing with academic pressure?"

1. What kind of a student were you in high school? With which of these students do you identify most? Do you think your academic experience colors your attitudes toward school issues? Explain your answer.

2. Does your ministry offer tutoring for students in need of additional help to succeed in school? Why or why not?

3. Make a list of factors that you believe contribute to students' academic success or struggles. Brainstorm ministry ideas and teaching topics that could help address as many of these issues as possible.

4. Someone once said, "Your grades are a testimony to your relationship with Christ." Do you agree or disagree with this statement? Explain your answer.

5. Is it possible for students or parents to put too much emphasis on grades? If so, have you ever observed or experienced this firsthand? What might the implications of this be on a student's spiritual growth?

6. What would you say to a student who seems to have an unhealthy obsession with his or her grades and GPA?

7. What would you say to a student who doesn't seem to care about academic success at all?

8. Have you ever used youth group time to teach about study skills? If so, what Scriptures did you use?

9. On a scale of 1 to 10, how knowledgeable are you about different learning styles? How much do you know about learning disorders or disabilities? Where could you find more information?

10. List ten personal study tips that have helped you in the past. Which of these could you share with the students in your ministry?

BREAKING UP

As you turn the corner, you come upon a teary-eyed freshman girl talking to one of your adult volunteers. Once you are a little closer, you hear the student say, "I can't believe he broke up with me, after all we've meant to each other during the last three weeks—and right before Valentine's Day, too!"

The student abruptly departs and you're left face-to-face with the volunteer. "Can you believe how shaken up she was about getting dumped by a boyfriend?" You know she'll get over it, but you also know her pain is very real. The situation sets your mind to reflecting on the power of relationships in the lives of students.

1. What would you say to a student who's obviously distraught over the breakup of a relationship? How would those words have sounded to you the last time you were left hurting by an ended relationship?

2. What Scripture (if any) would you share with a heartbroken student who came to you for counsel? Explain your thinking.

3. Do you think it's valuable for students to conduct a "personal relationship inventory" prior to starting a new relationship as a way of helping to address issues that have caused past breakups? Why or why not? If so, which of the following issues would you invite students to consider?

   - Poor communication
   - Insensitivity
   - Possessiveness
   - Selfishness
   - Too physical
   - Disrespect
   - Ego
   - Dishonesty

4. What steps can you take to help prevent students' breakups from negatively affecting the dynamics in your youth ministry?

5. How often do you teach on the subject of dating and relationships? What resources have you found helpful? What books would you recommend for students to read on their own?

6. Consider the following possible emotional responses that a breakup might produce in a jilted student. How will you help students deal with each of these?

   - Anger
   - Self-centeredness
   - Loss of self-esteem
   - Anxiety
   - Depression
   - Emptiness
   - Bitterness
   - Grief

7. Some youth leaders have suggested that our culture's current dating practices teach students more about how to get divorced than about how to build healthy marriages and relationships. Do you think dating is a failed idea? What would you propose as an alternative?

"I HATE MY PARENTS!"

"I hate my parents! My mom never lets me do anything! She won't even listen to my requests!" The kid sitting before you, Jeff, is a good guy, but it's obvious his relationship with his parents is strained. "My dad is gone so much because of his job—it's like we never talk except when he yells at me for something!" You wonder how Jeff's parents would respond if they were sitting in front of you. You suspect you're not getting the whole story. But for now, you take a deep breath as you think about what you'll say to Jeff about how to have a winning relationship with his parents.

1. What was your relationship like with your own parents when you were a teenager? What would you do differently if you could go back and relive those years?

2. What issues do you detect in Jeff's lament about his parents? How would you respond to him? Are there any questions you'd want to discuss with his parents? Why or why not?

3. What are the most common sources of conflict between students and parents?

4. When was the last time you taught about building strong relationships with parents? What Scriptures did you use? What might you do to improve your teaching on the topic?

5. Does your ministry provide any classes or training for parents on parenting adolescents? Why or why not? If you do provide such instruction, what material do you cover? What are your goals?

6. Some degree of tension between parents and teenagers is a normal part of the process of growing up. What signs would you look for that might indicate family conflict that needs to be referred to specialized professional help?

7. Dr. Les Parrott has stated, "When parents are not getting along with each other, teenagers feel threatened, afraid, and angry. Unstable homes are a significant cause of adolescent rebellion against parents."[18] Respond to this quotation and its possible counseling implications.

---

18. Les Parrott, *Helping Your Struggling Teenager* (Grand Rapids, MI: Zondervan, 2000), 277.

CREATION CARE

When you walk into the church kitchen on a Sunday evening, you find two of your students in the midst of a rather heated discussion. "I can't believe you don't recycle! I just saw you dump aluminum cans in the trash. Doesn't Genesis talk about how we're supposed to take care of creation?"

The accused student doesn't give an inch: "Frankly, I think putting aluminum cans in a separate container and then transporting them all to a recycling center every couple of weeks takes more time and energy than it saves. And I think some kids in our group are more interested in recycling a few cans than they are in sharing the gospel!"

The two students turn to you for a response. What would you say?

1. Does your ministry recycle? Why or why not?
2. Do you view care of the creation as a Christian priority? Why or why not?

ON DEATH AND DYING

The text arrived while you were eating breakfast: "This is Jessie and Megan. Please come to the hospital as soon as you can! We're in the waiting room on the third floor. Hurry!" You and your group have been praying for Jessie and Megan's grandfather for the past several weeks during your youth meetings. As you drive to the hospital, you send up a prayer for God's help and guidance. When you step off the elevator on the third floor, you instantly see Jessie, Megan, and the family. Jessie gives you an update on their grandfather: "Late last night, Grandpa went into a coma and was placed on a ventilator. But his brain scan indicates no brain wave activity. In his living will Grandpa said he wanted no extraordinary measures to resuscitate or keep him alive because his cancer is so advanced. We are all so tired, worried, and emotional—and we're about to sit down with doctors and the hospital chaplain. Will you come to that meeting with us and help us think about what God would want us to do?"

1. Would you agree to attend the meeting? Why or why not? If you attend, what would you see as your role?
2. Have you ever been involved in a similar situation involving questions about death? If so, describe your emotions and decisions at the time.
3. Based on your understanding of science and Scripture, when does life end and death begin? When the hearts stops beating on its own? When the brain ceases functioning? When natural respiration ceases? When medically produced respiration and heartbeat end? At some other time?
4. What medical factors would need to be present for you to decide to remove a respirator?
5. Would your decision regarding the removal or non-removal of a respirator be affected by whether the person is a Christian or not? Explain your answer.

6. Is withholding or not providing food and water ever acceptable as a way of shortening the suffering of a terminally ill patient?
7. In what ways have advances in medical science complicated traditional understandings of death and dying?

FUNERAL FOR A PET

"My dog, Sadie, died on Friday, and I want to have a funeral for her," says fifteen-year-old Kristi, with tears in her eyes. "She'd been with me since I was three years old. She was there by my side through my parents' divorce. Honestly, she was my best friend. Would you be willing to help me plan a memorial service for her—and maybe come and say a prayer? It'll probably just be me and my mom, but it'd mean a lot to us."

1. Will you help plan and perform such a funeral? Why or why not?
2. If yes, what would the service include?
3. Do animals go to heaven?
4. Do animals have "souls"? Explain your answer.
5. What else could you do to help Kristi in her time of sadness?

THE ABORTION DEBATE

A student stands in the doorway of your office with a deeply troubled facial expression. "We're doing debates in my speech class this semester, and I've been assigned the topic of abortion. My teacher says I need to be prepared to argue either side of the issue. I've never really thought a lot about the topic, and I can't decide whether to look at it from a legal, historical, moral, ethical, medical, or theological perspective—or all of them. Plus, I've always thought the big question was about when life begins, so I was gonna focus on that—but my friend says that's not even the real issue! What do you think? And do you think it's okay for me to argue both sides, even if it's just for a class? I really need your advice!"

1. What would you say to this student?
2. What specific books or other resources do you have on hand to share with youth who seek your advice on this topic? What websites or other resources would you recommend—including people a student might speak with?
3. What biblical passages would you highlight to help illuminate this issue for a student?
4. Is the critical issue "When does life begin?" Explain your answer.
5. What would you tell your students about how to interact with those who disagree with your perspective on this issue?

CHRISTLIKE DISAGREEMENT

"I really need your help!" The sheepish smile on the face of one of your favorite students belies the serious nature of her concern. "I'm really embracing your challenge to talk with my non-Christian friends about Jesus. But it seems like no matter what I do, every conversation about God that I try to have with my unchurched friends ends up in an argument. Even when I "win" the debate, the other person ends up angry with me, and I walk away wondering if I've really fulfilled Christ's purposes. I guess I'm wondering what I'm doing wrong. I mean, it seems like Jesus talked about a lot of controversial subjects with all different kinds of people, and some ended up following him and others walked away angry. But Jesus knew he was saying what needed to be said—I'm not always so sure! Do you think communicating like Jesus means focusing on the content of the conversation or the style or both? How do I keep every serious conversation I have with a non-Christian from turning into an argument?"

1. How would you answer this student?
2. How would you explain the idea of a Christ-like dialogue?
3. Have you ever "won a debate" with a person that had a significant impact on that person's spiritual life? Explain your answer.
4. What theological subjects seem to lead to arguments most often? Does this mean these subjects should be avoided? Explain your answer.
5. Is it possible to speak truth in an untruthful way? Explain your answer.
6. Define your thoughts about the role of listening when you are in dialogue with a person with whom you fundamentally disagree.
7. State some concrete ways you seek to demonstrate Christ's love, a humble attitude, and a servant's heart when disagreeing with someone.
8. Proverbs 15:1 reads, "A gentle answer turns away wrath, but a harsh word stirs up anger." How would you explain to a student what the word *gentle* means in this context?

DISCERNING GOD'S WILL

"I just can't decide which college to attend," Susan said, when she met with you at the local coffee shop. "There are so many things to consider! How can I figure out what God wants for me?" As you look back at her over the top of your cup of espresso, all the personal wrestling you've done with determining God's will for you comes to mind. How will you respond to Susan's question in a way that will both speak to her questions and honor God and his Word?

1. Think back over your own experiences in discerning God's will for you. How successful were your efforts? What was most helpful to you in the process? What would you recommend to Susan? What have you tried that you absolutely would not recommend?

2. Explain how you understand the role of each of the following items in discerning God's will:

    - Prayer
    - Scripture
    - Reason
    - Wise counsel
    - Imagination
    - Quiet listening
    - Christian peers
    - WWJD?
    - Circumstances
    - Spiritual gifts
    - Feelings

3. It's estimated that the average person makes between 300 and 17,000 decisions every day. How do you decide which choices are important enough to reflect upon deeply and which can be made with little or no reflection? Do you believe that God has a specific will for every decision you make—no matter how large or small?

4. What particular Scripture passages would you draw on if you were to teach a series on "Discovering God's Will"?

5. What books or resources on making decisions have you found helpful enough to recommend to others?

6. The book of Proverbs says, "Plans fail for lack of counsel, but with many advisers they succeed (15:22). When seeking support in making a big decision, what qualities do you look for in a wise advisor or counselor?

4

THE BIBLE, THEOLOGY, AND CHRISTIAN EDUCATION

GOD SPEAKS

Your newest staff member steps into your office and says, "God spoke to me and told me we need to sign the high school group up for the Haiti mission trip this summer." She stands in front of you, expecting an answer. When you don't respond immediately, she seems confused: "God *does* speak to you, doesn't he? How else do you know what to teach on and what you'll say when you stand in front of the group?" You pause for a moment to collect your thoughts, fire up a brief prayer to God, and invite her to have a seat so you can talk about it . . .

1. What would your initial response be to this staff member who expects you to act on her suggestion immediately because God told her what the group needs to do?
2. How do you think God communicates with people today?
3. Have you ever experienced God clearly speaking to you in the way this staff member describes? If so, how did you communicate this experience to others? How did they respond?
4. What Scriptures would you use if you were to teach a group of students on the topic of "God speaking"?
5. What are the advantages or disadvantages of a completely "supernatural" understanding of how God speaks to us today? What are the advantages and disadvantages of a completely "rational" understanding of how God speaks to us?
6. Do spiritual gifts such as prophecy, tongues, interpretation, and words of wisdom enter into this discussion? Explain your answer.

"THAT'S WHAT IT MEANS TO ME"

Your senior-high Bible study is going great. Students are engaged, asking great questions and sharing observations about Jesus' Sermon on the Mount. You're really pleased with how things are moving, until Chris, a sophomore guy on your right, proclaims authoritatively: "Matthew 6:5-6 clearly states that our praying in a circle after Bible study is against Jesus' teaching! It's too public! It's obvious that Jesus only wants us to pray in private. Anyway, *that's what it means to me*." Other students immediately begin chiming in, offering their own perspectives, other teachings they've heard on the passage, and notes from their study Bibles. As you raise your hand in hopes of stilling the youth enough to speak to the important questions they're raising, Chris's words ring in your ears: "That's what it means to me."

1. How would you address Chris's concern about Matthew 6:5-6 and the Bible study prayer circle?
2. How would you speak to the rather common situation of students explaining the meaning of a particular Scripture by simply saying, "Well, that's what it means to me"?
3. Do you try to teach students about basic principles of biblical interpretation in your youth ministry? Why or why not?
4. What basic concepts do people need to understand in order to interpret the Scriptures responsibly? What resources could you recommend to students that have helped you in this area?
5. Does "requiring" youth to seek out the meaning a text had for its original audience in its original context "scare" students away from exploring the Bible on their own? Explain your answer.

PROMISES, PROMISES, PROMISES

The message light on your desk phone is flashing as you arrive at your office early on a Wednesday morning. You pick up the phone to hear a message from Jill, a ninth-grader in your group. "Hi, it's Jill. In small group last night, our leader read a few Scriptures that have been bothering me all night, and I was hoping you could help me out. The first was Proverbs 22:6 which says that if parents raise children well, their kids won't turn away from God. I have an older cousin who recently died. He was raised by godly parents but rejected God. Why didn't God keep his promise? Hitting even closer to home, we looked at Matthew 7:7 and Christ's promises about prayer. I prayed for my cousin to repent, but he never did. Can you tell me why God sometimes breaks the promises he makes in Scripture? Please call— this is driving me crazy." As you hang up the phone, your mind is already beginning to work on how you view the promises of God.

1. How would you respond to Jill regarding the two specific passages she raised?
2. Is it correct to understand a biblical proverb like the one Jill quotes as a promise from God? Why or why not? How do the different genres of biblical literature affect the way Scripture is understood?
3. How would you explain to a ninth-grader the difference between the conditional promises from God that appear in Scripture and God's unconditional promises? Can you think of an example of each?
4. Are Old Testament prophesies different from New Testament promises? If so, how would you explain the difference?
5. What other biblical "promises" can you think of that students might get confused about? How would you explain them in a youth ministry context?

COLLEGE FAITH CRISIS

"I can't believe you never told me about this stuff when I was in youth group." Pat pauses to take a breath, and then his accusatory tone continues with more force. "I took a course on 'The Bible as Literature' at the university, figuring it'd be all stuff I knew since I've been in the church my whole life. And then I find out from my professor that many scholars believe Moses didn't really write any of the Old Testament and that Job may not have been an actual person. He even says that the Gospels may represent what the second-century church thought about Jesus, not what actually happened as recorded by eyewitnesses. Do you really believe in the Bible in light of current scholarship? After what I've learned in college, I sure don't!"

1. How would you respond to Pat?
2. What resources would you recommend to students who have questions about the history, authorship, and authority of the Bible?
3. Have you ever talked to a former youth ministry student who had an experience similar to Pat's? If you've been to college and/ or seminary, how was your personal experience similar to Pat's? Different?
4. How do you currently prepare students for the questions and struggles they may encounter if they are exposed to different scholarly approaches to the Bible?
5. Do you stay up to date on biblical scholarship? If so, how? If not, why not?
6. How have your own views about the Bible changed since you were in high school?

FOUR-CORNERS DEFENSE

Your senior-high Bible study is looking at a beautiful section of prophesy from Isaiah 11. All is going well, until you get to the verse which tells of how the Lord will gather the scattered peoples from "the four corners of the earth" (11:12) "So, wait a minute," Jason interrupts. "You mean to tell me that Isaiah is speaking for God, but he thinks the world is flat?" How would you respond to Jason—and to the larger question of whether the Bible is authoritative in matters of science?

MEMORIZING SCRIPTURE

Mr. Perry was really a great guy, except for the fact that he brought up the same topic every time he chatted with you. "So how is it going integrating Bible memorization into the youth ministry? I was reading in Joshua 1:8 again this morning, and it talks about how God will bless those who memorize his Word. I sure do want to see God bless that great group of students you work with in your ministry. And there are all kinds of different Bible-memory programs available now, so you don't even have to design the program yourself. That should be a real time-saver." You smile as you formulate your response.

1. What will you say in response to Mr. Perry's question? What will you say when he asks again next month?
2. How much Scripture have you memorized personally? In what translation? How has this shaped your own faith?
3. What are three common reasons students give for not memorizing Scripture? What reasons do youth workers give?
4. Think about how you would respond to a youth who asked the following questions about getting started memorizing Scripture:

   • Which translation should I use?
   • What Scriptures should I start with?
   • How many verses should I try to memorize each week?
   • How can I retain past verses while memorizing new verses?
   • What benefits can I expect to experience in my spiritual life?
   • What books or other resources can help me?

5. Do you see memorizing the Bible as an essential part of faith development for young Christians? On a scale of 1 to 10, how important to your youth ministry is teaching students to memorize Scripture? Explain your answer.
6. What dangers, if any, do you see in emphasizing Bible memorization in youth ministry? Explain your answer.

LOST IN TRANSLATION?

"But which one is the Word of God? They can't *all* be right." That's the comment one student makes after you go around the Bible study circle, inviting each of your eleventh-graders to read a different translation of a particular verse. Suddenly, the handful of students who'd been less than fully engaged in your study of Luke 2 are eager to hear your response. How do you explain the intricacies of various translations without getting kids bogged down in the details?

DISCERNING STUDENTS' SPIRITUAL GIFTS

"Hey, can we try doing one of those spiritual-gift inventory thingies?" says one of your students as the group is gathering for Bible study one night. You smile, as she continues: "My friend from school said his group was discussing the gifts of the Spirit and they all went online and answered these questions, and each person got a printout that listed his or her gifts. Isn't that cool? How did people find out their spiritual gifts before the Internet? Do they have these questions in a book somewhere? Is that how you found out what your gift was? My friend said one of the gifts he scored highest on is a gift he isn't even sure he really understands. Are these things always accurate? When can we try it?" As her questions wind down, you begin thinking again about how you'll handle the rich but somewhat charged topic of spiritual gifts.

1. What are the strengths and weaknesses of standardized spiritual gift inventories?

2. In what other ways might you encourage students to discover and discern their spiritual gifts?

3. What are the pluses and minuses of adolescents seeking to discern their spiritual gifts even as they are growing, maturing, and discovering who they are?

4. Do spiritual gifts change over the course of a person's life depending on need in the Body of Christ? Explain your answer.

5. What books, resources, websites or curricula do you trust and use with students when studying spiritual gifts?

6. Should the passages that list spiritual gifts in the New Testament (Romans 12, 1 Corinthians 12, Ephesians 4, and 1 Peter 4) be considered "descriptive" (partial) lists or "exhaustive" (comprehensive) lists that include all gifts for all times?

7. Brainstorm what you believe to be the top five questions your students have about spiritual gifts. How will you address each one?

TEENAGE MENTORS

Stephen is sitting in front of you with an iced coffee in hand and an intent look on his face: "I've been asked to mentor an elementary school student this semester," he says. "I'm excited about having the chance to help somebody, but I'm not sure I really know what the term *mentoring* means, even though I've heard it a lot. I mean, how is it different from tutoring or just being a friend? And how do you select a person to mentor? And what do you do when you meet together?" How would you answer Stephen?

ON GIFTS AND FRUIT

As you lie awake, you find yourself replaying the conversation from the evening's staff meeting:

Shawn: I think we're going to have to ask him to leave the ministry team!

Pat: But if we remove him from the team, our teaching will really suffer. He is the most gifted volunteer teacher and leader we've had in this ministry in a long time. I don't know how we'd replace him.

Shawn: But time after time we see such immature behavior from him—including jealousy, gossip, and fits of rage. He's incredibly difficult to work with. Despite his amazing gifts, I just don't feel like the love and joy of the Spirit is very apparent in his ministry.

Pat: I don't disagree. But look how the ministry is growing. People are flocking to be taught and led by him. His behavior is far from stellar, but I think we need to give him a break. Maybe this is an opportunity for *us* to display a little grace, given all the pressure surrounding the rapid growth of the ministry.

Shawn: It is amazing how the Spirit sometimes seems to give such important gifts to people who aren't very focused on exhibiting the fruit of the Spirit that Paul describes in Galatians 5.

1. Have you ever faced a ministry situation in which spiritual gifts were more in evidence than spiritual fruit? Explain how you dealt with that situation.

2. Consider your own ministry in light of the fruit of the Spirit described in Galatians 5:22-23. Which of these fruit have you seen growing most in your own life and ministry this year? Which fruit will you focus on developing more fully in the next year?

3. Does spiritual maturity come about through the exercise of the Spirit's gifts, or is the exercise of one's gifts a privilege that should be based on evidence of the Spirit's fruit? Explain your answer.

4. What kind of process would you suggest as a way of restoring a gifted ministry practitioner who is "caught in a sin" (Galatians 6:1). Note that the Greek word translated "restore" can refer to setting bones for proper healing, mending fishing nets, or bringing together disagreeing factions.

YOUR TEACHING PRIORITIES

As you gaze at the blank calendar for the coming year, you begin to worry. The seminar on advanced planning at last fall's youth ministry conference urged youth workers not to just pick whatever topic most suited their interests on a particular week but to ask the hard question—"What do I most want my students to learn over the course of their youth ministry experience?"—and then plan the teaching calendar accordingly. You've diligently sought out advice from more seasoned youth workers, but now it's your job to pick up the pen and fill in the calendar. But where do you start?

1. List up to ten essential topics that you believe are important enough that you want to be sure to teach about them every year in your ministry. Explain your answer!

2. Make a second list of topics that might not be a central issue every year, but that you'd definitely want to teach on at some point during the four years each high school student is involved in your ministry.

3. Weigh the importance of teaching on the following topics by listing how many weeks (if any) you would expect to devote to each:

   _____ Abortion
   _____ Apostles' Creed
   _____ Baptism
   _____ Church History
   _____ Creation/Evolution
   _____ Denominational Distinctives
   _____ Divorce
   _____ Eschatology
   _____ Getting Along with Parents
   _____ Love, Sex, and Dating
   _____ Other World Religions
   _____ Materialism/Greed
   _____ Pornography

_____ Prayer

_____ Vocation

4. What topics are more important for middle school students? What topics are specific to high school students? Why?
5. What essential biblical passages, themes, or characters need to be taught about every year?
6. How many weeks would you plan to spend teaching on "holiday themes" each year? Explain your answer!

TEACHING ON TOUGH TOPICS

Your palms are still drenched in sweat as you finish your talk about the very painful topic of cutting and self-injury among teenagers. After you close the meeting in prayer, several students rush up to you to express their appreciation for your willingness to tackle a subject they'd never heard addressed from a biblical perspective. You're aware that your comments may result in phone calls from a few concerned parents, but you're convinced it's worth it—because these are the kinds of real-life issues your students and their peers are wrestling with every day.

1. Identify ten important-yet-possibly-controversial subjects that you believe your students need to hear addressed from a Christian perspective.

2. What steps can you take in advance to minimize negative feedback when teaching on controversial subjects? With staff? With parents? With students?

3. When you teach on troubling subjects or those where Christians may disagree, do you present only your own perspective or do you seek to present multiple views? What are the pluses and minuses of each approach?

4. What are the strengths and weaknesses of utilizing guest speakers to address controversial subjects?

5. Are there any "trendy" issues that you would not want to address in a youth ministry teaching context, even though your students might find them interesting? Explain your selections.

6. How do you respond to a parent or staff member's concern about your choosing to address controversial topics with students— especially if that adult disagrees with your perspective?

BEYOND BUNNIES AND BASKETS

As you walk through the mall with a couple of students, one of them comments on the increased commercialization of Easter. "I know we're stuck with the fact that stores now start putting Christmas decorations up in October, but now it seems to be happening at Easter, as well."

"Yeah," the other student chimes in. "The resurrection gets buried under Easter candy, baskets, and brunches. Every store has Easter sales, and lots of homes put up bunny outdoor decorations. It seems even church youth and children's programs get caught up in the commercialization. What do you think we should be doing in our ministry to keep the resurrection at the center of Easter?" What would you say to these students?

REPETITION

As you stand sipping a much-needed cup of coffee after what you thought was a solid youth gathering, you hear a group of students chatting as they walk toward the door. Engaged in conversation, they are totally unaware of your presence, even though you can hear every word they're saying. The conversation drifts toward the youth ministry teaching time, and you are shocked by what you hear: "Did you hear the topic for next week. I can't believe it. We just talked about that last summer!"

"Yeah," his friend agrees. "I can't wait to hear about something new. It seems we just go over the same thing again and again. It's getting *boring*."

You walk away shaking your head. Isn't repetition the key to learning?

1. On a scale of 1 to 10, rate how much you agree with the idea that repetition is the key to learning. Explain your answer.
2. What topics are so essential that they must be repeated on a regular basis?
3. How do you teach repeatedly on key subjects without becoming boring?
4. What are the strengths and weaknesses of teaching on a particular topic more than once a year when working with middle school students? What about high school students?

TEACHER RECRUITMENT

It happens around the same time every year. You notice it first in the way people seem to avoid eye contact with you as you walk down the hallways. It continues as people seem unwilling to return your phone calls or respond to email. Every year, it seems harder and harder to recruit new teachers and provide them the training they need to be effective. The annual recruitment ritual leads you to ponder some important issues about the teachers involved in your ministry.

1. What do you look for in a teacher? What particular qualifications are you looking for in someone you would recruit to teach students?
2. What are the most frequent "excuses" you've heard from potential teachers? How do you respond to each of these objections?
3. How often do you provide training for teachers? What was included in your last teacher-training session?
4. What is one book or resource you would like to see all of your teachers read before they begin teaching? Explain your answer.
5. Do you have a written job description for teachers in your ministry? Why or why not?
6. What strategies have you found to be most successful in recruiting new teachers?
7. Brainstorm at least ten things your ministry could do to help encourage and retain its current teachers.
8. Do you have a way of formally evaluating the effectiveness of your teachers? If so, how do you conduct the evaluation? How frequently are teachers evaluated?

SUNDAY SCHOOL

"I can't believe you're talking about canceling Sunday school! Don't you care about Christian education at all?" This email from a concerned mom is pretty typical of the reactions you've had from several parents after suggesting that the church might want to rethink its youth programming on Sunday mornings. As you sit down at your desk to reconsider the possibility, you close your eyes and let your mind wander back to the thought process that led to your original recommendation.

1. What are the strengths and weaknesses of utilizing Sunday school as a primary vehicle for Christian education?

2. Brainstorm at least six other options for how Christian education might be handled.

    A) _____
    B) _____
    C) _____
    D) _____
    E) _____
    F) _____

Outline the strengths and weaknesses of each of these options.

3. Is there a better use of the time with youth on Sunday mornings than a traditional Sunday school? If so, what?

4. When you brought the topic up at a recent lunch with other youth pastors, one colleague said, "Sunday school is such an out-of-date term that it gets in the way. Just using the word *school* turns off non-churched students." Do you agree or disagree? Explain your answer.

5. Another colleague insists: "If it's done with excellence, Sunday school can still have as much impact on students today as it has in previous generations." Agree or disagree?

6. In what ways are your current Christian education practices like "school" (desks, assignments, workbooks, etc.)? In what ways are they totally different?

MEASURING TEACHING EFFECTIVENESS

At your youth ministry staff meeting, your two colleagues were at odds on the topic of measuring teaching effectiveness. "There's just no way we can objectively evaluate our teachers and the degree to which they're helping our youth grow spiritually," said Chris, who oversees the middle school ministry.

But David, who leads the senior high group, was equally passionate about his own perspective: "There *must* be a way to measure ongoing maturity and Christian teaching effectiveness. If we can't assess how we're doing, how can we ever improve? Many ministries use inadequate standards, but that doesn't mean there aren't ways to measure how we're doing."

After a moment of silence, your two frustrated coworkers turn to you. "Well, as the leader of this ministry, you must have an opinion," David said.

"Yeah, you've been awfully quiet," said Chris. "What do you think?"

Recognizing that the issue of measuring spiritual growth and teaching effectiveness is obviously a controversial subject among your staff, you measure your words carefully as you respond . . .

1. Do you agree more with Chris or David? Why?
2. What are some *ineffective* ways ministries try to measure spiritual maturity and teaching effectiveness? List as many as you can.
3. How do you know when you have been successful in teaching a group of students?
4. Do you stress "learning objectives" and "measurable outcomes" when you teach or delegate teaching responsibilities to others? Why or why not?
5. What was the most recent major change you made in your teaching approach? How did you discover the need for a change?
6. Have you ever video-recorded one of your teaching sessions so you could watch yourself and improve your presentation skills? If so, what did you learn?

BEHAVIOR MANAGEMENT

"I'm sorry—but I quit!" Those are the first words you hear from one of your newest volunteers as she steps through the door of your office on a Monday morning. For the past six weeks, she's been leading a small group of tenth-graders on Sunday evenings. "This group of students has no self-control, no interest in learning, and they refuse to stop talking." As you attempt to elicit more details on the problem, it becomes clear that the primary behavior issue concerns Kelly, who serves as an instigator for the other students. At the end of a long meeting, your volunteer sums up her situation as she departs: "Well, I'll continue leading this group, but only if Kelly is not allowed back for a couple of weeks. And then if she comes back and continues to be a major problem, I'll need to ask her to leave."

1. Would you agree to ban Kelly from coming to the small group meeting next week as your volunteer suggested? Why or why not?
2. What are the advantages and disadvantages of continuing to allow a disruptive student like Kelly to continue to attend meetings even if her behavior issues are not completely resolved?
3. How would you summarize your basic philosophy on discipline for students with unruly and distracting behavior?
4. At what point, if any, would you contact parents about disruptive behavior in a small group setting?
5. At what point, if any, would you send a student home or ask him or her not to come to future meetings?
6. List five types of student disruptions you commonly encounter. How would you instruct a volunteer to deal with each one?
7. How could you help a volunteer see past the day-to-day discipline issues and consider some of the possible underlying issues in Kelly's life?

5

RECREATION, RETREATS, AND ROAD TRIPS

NOT JUST FUN AND GAMES

"If I *never* have to lead another game, that'll be too soon!" a youth leader sitting next to you laments.

"Yeah," agrees another youth worker across the table from you. "I'm sure glad youth ministry has moved beyond being all about fun and games and now focuses on meeting students' *real* needs by going deeper. All that time we used to waste on recreation is now ministry-focused."

"Well, I'd argue that youth ministry has never been just about fun and games," offered one seasoned youth ministry veteran. "Games are a way of building relationships and connections among youth and also between kids and adults. They can be a real ministry in and of themselves."

"I totally agree," another youth pastor commented. "Besides, with students so stressed out and pressured by school, if we don't teach them to have fun and play, where are they going to learn it?" All eyes turn to you as the only youth worker at the table who's not yet shared a perspective on the role of games in youth ministry.

1. How would you respond to this group of fellow youth workers?
2. Why do you think games and recreation have a "bad reputation" in some youth ministry circles?
3. How would you describe the role of games and recreation in your philosophy of youth ministry?
4. Compared with a year ago, are you now playing more games, fewer games, or about the same amount? If there's been a change, explain why.
5. Do you consider yourself to be good at leading games? What makes someone good at leading games?
6. Do you believe students today need to be taught how to play and have fun with others? Explain your answer.
7. Name your favorite youth ministry game. Name your least favorite. What do you like or dislike about these games?

8. What resources have you found most helpful in planning and leading games and recreation?
9. Do you consider leading students in games to be "real ministry"? Why or why not?

"I HATE THESE GAMES!"

"You don't get it! We hate these stupid games, and we won't come to youth group if you expect us to play!" The two defiant freshmen girls now glaring at you show no sign of backing down. All you'd done was walk over and encourage them to join in the evening's volleyball game. Although these freshmen consistently sit out of just about every game or other physical activities, they're actively involved in other ministry activities like service projects, worship, and small groups. Several other students have noticed the two girls' lack of participation and have tried to excuse themselves from playing, but so far you've been able to limit the number of kids who sit on the sidelines. However, you fear that if kids know they have the option of not participating, more and more students will sit out.

1. How would you handle this issue with these students in the moment? How would you follow up later?
2. Why do you think these students respond to games and recreational activities in this way?
3. What are the strengths and weaknesses of letting their decision not to participate go unchallenged?
4. Have you ever utilized multiple recreational options at the same event as a way of involving people of differing interests and talents? How did it go? What are the strengths and weaknesses of such an approach?
5. Are there any types of games and recreation that you particularly dislike? How have you avoided (or tried to avoid) playing those types of games in the past?
6. If these students agreed to take pictures of others playing and enjoying the games, would that be acceptable? Explain your answer.
7. What other options for "participating" have you offered to those who do not want to play?

THE THRILL OF COMPETITION

Getting called into your supervisor's office is never easy, especially when your ministry practices are being questioned. As you take a seat opposite the large desk, your supervisor declares: "I've had several calls from parents recently expressing concern about how competitive the youth ministry's games have become. Last Sunday night, one student's glasses were broken by a volleyball spike . . . from a staff member. A few weeks ago I overheard a very heated argument between students about whether one team had broken the rules of your video scavenger hunt. And in the fall, we had a broken window in the rec room and two insurance claims for injuries suffered during games that were supposedly "noncontact" in nature! You do a great job of planning fun games and activities, but this year your staff and students seem to be getting carried away. Can you find a way to tone down the competitive spirit a bit?" Your mind is in a whirl as you consider how you'll speak to these concerns.

1. How would you respond to your supervisor's concerns?
2. What signs would you look for that indicate that games and activities might be getting too competitive?
3. What lessons, if any, do you believe kids can learn from competition?
4. On a scale of 1 to 10, how competitive is the youth ministry you are currently working with?
5. Are there any games or activities that you no longer use because the players became too competitive?
6. How have you successfully lowered the intensity levels of games in the past? What have you tried that did not work?
7. Do you ever play noncompetitive cooperative-type games with your students? How do they respond?
8. Do you consider yourself competitive? Have you ever become too intense in a game with students? Describe how you handled the situation.

HAUNTED HOUSE

"I have a great idea for our fall outreach!" Jason, an energetic sopho-more, was the newest member of the student leadership team for your ministry. "In my last youth group we hosted a haunted house with scenes depicting the horror that can sometimes occur when people dis-obey God's principles. The best part was the last room, where we had a really scary scene of the final judgment—and then there were counselors who would lead the scared students in a prayer for salvation. It was scary and really fun to act in—and lots of students said it was really powerful. Can we do something like that here?" How would you respond to this student's suggestion?

VIOLENT GAMES

The ringing phone on your desk finally captures your full attention on the fifth ring. Glancing at the caller ID you see it's the father of two teenagers in your youth ministry. After some introductory pleasantries, he shares the real reason for the call. "My son and daughter came home last night and said they'd played a couple of games at youth group called 'Mafia' and 'Warlords'—and then they handed me the permission form for the 'Paintball Battle Royale' you are sponsoring later this month. I just don't understand why a ministry that lifts up the Prince of Peace would constantly use games that have such violent content and themes." How will you respond?

1. On a scale of 1 to 10, how sensitive would you say you are to concerns about violent themes and content in planning games and events? Explain your answer.
2. Are there any games you won't play with students because of violent themes?
3. Do you take students to play paintball or other games that involve "shooting" at one another? What are the potential strengths and weaknesses of your decision in this area?
4. How would you respond to a student who says, "The Bible is full of wars and battles and violence. If the Bible doesn't shy away from these things, why are we worried about *pretend* violence in our games?"
5. Why do you think violent themes are so popular in video games, movies, music, and other entertainment? Do you address this topic in your teaching? Why or why not?
6. Do you utilize violent video games in your ministry? If so, how? If not, why not?

ACTIVE LEARNING

You listen in fascination as the seminar leader at the youth worker convention continues to wax eloquent. "You should *never* just play a game! Your time with students is too short. Instead, every game and recreational event should serve the dual purpose of giving kids a fun time but also setting up the topic for the evening. Research shows that active learning is among the most impactful and memorable forms of learning. So, rather than just lecturing to students about how Satan prowls around like a ravenous lion looking for people to devour, your recreation activity might be a dodgeball game with lions against shepherds and sheep. Most of the students would be sheep, playing the game on all fours while trying to avoid a few 'lions' who can move around the whole area on two legs and take out the sheep with a well-placed toss of the ball. A few other kids would be shepherds who can throw themselves in front of the ball to protect the sheep any way they can. This sets up a discussion of how to avoid the real roaring lions in our lives and the role of Christian leaders in protecting their sheep from spiritual danger. My advice is to make every game a learning activity that teaches a lesson as kids play." As the workshop ends and you collect your personal items and shove them in your backpack, you can't stop thinking about active learning.

1. Does your ministry currently make use of active-learning strategies that use games and activities that teach? Why or why not?

2. What are the strengths and weaknesses of active-learning recreation activities?

3. Describe the most successful active-learning event you've led. What helped make it effective?

4. Why do you think some youth leaders are hesitant to use active-learning elements?

5. Do you think it is possible to overuse active-learning strategies? How would you know when you've reached a saturation point?

6. Brainstorm five biblical or theological concepts that you think could naturally lend themselves to active-learning activities? What themes would not be taught or illustrated effectively in these ways?

FOOD FIGHT!

At the pre-retreat meeting, the recreation director was offering a preview of the final evening's big event. "We're calling it The World's Largest Food Fight. Students and staff will be divided into two groups and gathered on opposite sides of the field. We'll supply 55-gallon drums of wet spaghetti noodles, eggs to throw, balloons filled with mustard and ketchup, marshmallows that can be dipped in chocolate sauce, and even surgical gloves filled with flour that can be shot over to the other side using the balloon launchers. It is going to be messy, crazy, fun, and something the students will never forget. Oh, and did we mention the Jell-O pit? Don't forget to bring your cameras and video recorders—it'll be great!"

As the leader sat down, a youth leader in the back row raised her hand tentatively. "Our group won't be attending that event. I have an ethical issue with wasting so much food when others in the world are starving. What does a game like that teach students about consumerism and what it means to live responsibly in a world where many people don't have what they need?"

Another hand went up, "Well, I think saying we shouldn't play food games feels a bit drastic and politically correct. Our group is really looking forward to the food fight. It sounds like a blast!"

How would you respond to this conversation? Would you and your group participate in "The World's Largest Food Fight?" Why or why not?

DANGEROUS GAMES

"Come on, flag football is for wimps," implore the wide-eyed students in front of you. "We want to play tackle in our annual Day-After-Thanksgiving Turkey Bowl. You won't let us play Chubby Bunnies anymore because you're worried somebody will choke. We can't ride horses or go tubing in the mountains during winter camp, because it's dangerous. You've even disbanded the shockseat! You're not much fun anymore—all you think about is safety. Don't you believe God can protect us?" You shake your head and smile as your students have turned the discussion into a theological debate yet again.

1. What would you say about students playing tackle football at a youth ministry event? Explain your answer.
2. What games do you avoid because the risk of injury is too great?
3. Have you ever checked the insurance policy of your church or ministry to see which activities are prohibited and, therefore, not covered under your policy? If so, were you surprised by any of the prohibitions?
4. What would you say to a person who argues that ministries don't need to worry too much about safety or liability issues because we can trust that God will take care of his own?

SAFETY FIRST?

As you sit with other local youth workers planning the high school ski retreat, a spirited discussion is taking place. "The ski resort doesn't require helmets, and only recommends them for boarders and skiers on its advanced slopes. Personally, I don't think they're comfortable, and I never wear one. Plus, I'm not sure they really make things safer—sometimes skiers and boarders wearing helmets get much more aggressive and are willing to take more risks because they think they're protected from injury, when they're really not!"

"I completely disagree," says the young youth worker on your right. "I think we should make them mandatory for all skiers, boarders, and inner tubers on the retreat. In fact, I think it's our responsibility to have extra helmets on hand that we can loan to students who forget theirs or don't own one."

Both leaders appeal to you for your opinion. What would you say regarding safety, ski helmets, and your upcoming ski retreat?

PICKING TEAMS

"All my life I've been chosen last. No matter how many time it happens, it still hurts more than I can put into words." The adult volunteer's pain is obvious from his facial expression. You'd been running late, so to save a few minutes you'd asked two senior guys to be captains and alternately pick to choose up teams for dodgeball. You hadn't given it another thought until you were confronted by your volunteer at the end of the meeting. "There must be a better way of selecting teams that doesn't highlight the difference between the athletic 'haves' and 'have-nots.' The way the teams were picked tonight was cruel and hurtful to students who were picked near the end." As you prepare to respond, you fight a slight feeling of defensiveness, even as you want to validate the feelings of your friend and colleague in ministry.

1. What would you say to this adult volunteer? Are these concerns legitimate? Explain your answer.
2. Were you ever the last person picked for a team? If so, how did that feel? If not, how do you imagine you'd have felt?
3. Describe how you usually select teams for games in your ministry.
4. What are the strengths and weaknesses of using the "numbering off" method for choosing teams?
5. Do you ever adjust teams in the middle of a game to correct athletic imbalance? Why or why not?
6. Take three minutes to brainstorm as many different creative ways of selecting teams as you can.
7. Have you ever placed restrictions on more athletic players (such as asking members of the baseball team to throw with their opposite hand in dodgeball) as a way to minimize their impact on a game? Explain your answer.

CAMP SCHOLARSHIPS

You can't believe the number of requests you've received from students requesting financial help so they can attend camp this summer. Looking over the applications, you know there's a wide variety of need among these families—and the requests come from "core kids" who've been part of your ministry for years as well as from names you don't even recognize. In past years, you've never needed a firm "policy" about how the scholarship funds are allocated, but this year feels different. But a number of questions fill your mind.

1. What primary criteria should a ministry use to determine who receives funds? Financial need? Ministry involvement? Other?
2. Does repeatedly providing scholarships to the same families lead to "entitlement" or "learned dependence"? If so, what can youth ministries do to avoid these negative side effects?
3. Should a ministry provide full scholarships or only partials? Explain your answer.
4. Should scholarships be linked to particular expectations regarding performance, behavior, or service?

TO SLEEP, PERCHANCE TO DREAM

The retreat schedules had just been distributed to the staff when a hand in the back row shoots up. "Is this schedule right? Does it really represent how much sleep we're expecting students will get? Seems like we've got both late-night activities and early-morning opportunities all week."

Then your college intern speaks up: "I read that a study of the basketball team at Stanford University found that when players got extra sleep they increased their three-point and free-throw shooting by 9 percent. With ten hours of sleep, they also showed increased cognitive functioning."[19]

Then an older voice chimes in: "We *always* run on less sleep on retreats. It's a tradition, the students expect it—and, of course, staying up late is fun!"

But a quiet voice to your right responds, "But the spiritual content of the retreat is really important. Shouldn't we require that students get enough sleep to allow for the maximum impact?"

1. How many hours of sleep do you plan for camps and retreats?
2. Do you consider your students "sleep deprived"?
3. Do you ever teach students about the importance of sleep?
4. Do you model healthy sleep patterns that you'd want your students to emulate?

---

19. Results from a study by Stanford researcher Cheri Mah, cited in Peter Keating, "The Numbers," *ESPN: The Magazine,* April 16, 2012, 10.

WHEN THE CUP RUNS OVER

It's never happened before, but the numbers in front of you don't lie. The fundraiser for your upcoming Mexico mission trip was a huge success, bringing in about three times as much as you'd expected. All the scholarship requests have been filled, and you've even been able to set aside an extra 10 percent to cover unexpected costs for the trip. But you still have cash left over, so you have a decision to make. Will you . . .

- Bank the money for future ministry needs?
- Give the extra funds to a family, church, or social agency in the Mexican community where you'll be serving?
- Allow students to vote on what other ministry or social cause they will donate the money to?

Be sure to think about how you will explain the reasoning behind your decision to the ministry treasurer, parents, and anyone else who might ask!

MISSION TRIP "RECRUITMENT"

"I really want my grandchildren to go with your group on your student mission trip this spring." The older deacon had buttonholed you in the hallway after worship one Sunday. "These kids don't go to church or have anything to do with 'religion,' but I've heard about the impact these trips have had on other students. I'll be glad to pay for the cost of the trip for them. I came to you personally, because I spoke with another youth worker in their area, and she wouldn't let my grandkids participate because their trip was only for 'discipleship students' who'd been very active in the ministry. I think getting these kids out of their comfort zone might help them see the kind of difference Christ could make in their lives. You will take my grandkids on your trip, won't you?"

1. How would you respond to this request?
2. What are the benefits and drawbacks of viewing mission trips primarily in terms of how they affect the lives of the students who participate?

OLDER VS. YOUNGER VOLUNTEERS

When the church secretary hands you the volunteer applications for adult leaders at this year's middle school summer camp program, you're pleased to see the number of applicants. You begin by dividing them into four piles. In the first pile are applicants ages 18-24; the second includes ages 25-35; the third is ages 36-55; the fourth, ages 56 and up. As you begin reading over the first group, your ministry intern enters the office. Seeing the piles, he begins to laugh: "You're not seriously considering having retired people work at the middle school camp, are you? They don't have the energy of younger adults, and they don't have a clue about youth culture today. What could they possibly bring to the table?

1. How would you respond to this intern's comments and questions?
2. What are the strengths and weaknesses that each of these age groups might bring to the camp?
3. What benefits do you see in inviting older people to participate as volunteers in your ministry? How does it benefit the kids in the ministry? The volunteers? The larger church?
4. If you were to accept retirement-age persons as volunteers, what roles would you see them ideally suited to fill?
5. If you were to use older adolescents as volunteers for the middle school camp, what roles would you want them to fill?

BIG PROBLEMS AT BREAKFAST

Your eyes are barely open as you rummage through the plastic bags on the counter of the church kitchen, looking for the pancake mix. Glancing up at the clock, you see that it's 5:59 a.m. Since breakfast is scheduled to begin in an hour, you call in to the young man setting tables in the other room: "Hey, where's that pancake batter you bought? We've got to get those flapjacks going—we're gonna have a horde of hungry kids waking up soon."

The sound of silence greets your question, but when you look up you see an agonized expression on his face. "Oh, no, I completely forgot. The store was out of the instant batter you wanted, so I bought everything else and was going to go back and pick up the mix later. But then the week got so busy and . . ."

1. What are your next words to your young helper?
2. Brainstorm solutions that you and the young man might enact to save the breakfast.
3. How will you follow up on this teachable moment?
4. How would it change your response if the young man were a student leader? A college intern? A volunteer? The newest member of your ministry staff?

HAPPY BIRTHDAY!

As you leave your favorite lunch spot, you're hailed by an unfamiliar voice, "Hi, I wanted to introduce myself. I'm Cindy, the new youth pastor at First Church, and my friend told me that you're the local youth ministry 'expert.' Can I ask you a quick question?" Before you have a chance to respond, she continues: "I have four birthdays among the kids in my youth ministry this week. So, do you know any creative ways to celebrate birthdays? I mean, how do you celebate birthdays in your youth ministry? Does anyone ever question the amount of time or money you spend? If so, what do you say? I don't mean to pester you. Maybe now that I know where you like to eat lunch, I can buy you lunch next time." What would you say to your new friend?

6

WORSHIP, PRAYER, AND EVANGELISM

WORSHIP WARS

While standing in line for coffee between Sunday services, you happen to overhear a conversation between two older members of your congregation about the music in that day's worship service.

"I just don't understand the irreverent rock music that's crept into our church services lately—and why does it need to be played so loud?"

"I don't like it either, but it's way better than those 7-11 praise songs we've been singing—7 words repeated 11 times. Why don't we ever sing the classic hymns I grew up with?"

"All these songs make Jesus sound like the object of someone's infatuation rather than our divine Savior and Lord."

"Yes, and is an occasional Bach fugue too much to hope for?"

Fuming about their lack of flexibility, you make your way to the youth room just in time to hear a couple of high school students complaining.

"Why don't we ever have any decent music in church? It's always so slow and boring."

"They haven't played a David Crowder song in forever. Why don't we use the songs we use in youth group?"

"Why are all the hymns so full of strange language? I mean—'Here I raise my Ebenezer'? What the heck does that mean? I don't even know what those old songs are about half the time!"

"Yeah, and if we did some gospel hip-hop once in a while, it'd make it a lot easier to invite my friends to church . . ."

You continue down the hall, shaking your head over all you've just heard—and wondering what you could possibly say to help bridge the gap between these perspectives.

1. Do you think the youth you work with are in danger of becoming as entrenched in their own worship preferences as some older people seem to be? Why or why not?

2. How can a youth ministry teach appreciation of widely diverse approaches to praise and worship?

3.   What is your preferred style of worship? How open are you personally to other worship styles and traditions? What styles do you most dislike? Why?

PARTICIPATION VS. QUALITY

As you open the door to the youth room, your ears are immediately assaulted by the noise emanating from the youth praise-and-worship band. You catch the eye of the leader of the group, who grimaces slightly as she approaches you. "It's tough," she says. "Most of the band members are so young, and some of them haven't been playing very long. But some of the older students can't make the time commitment to attend both rehearsal and the required band Bible studies. Plus, these kids really want to offer their music to God. Who am I to say they don't play well enough?" You are tempted to relax the standards you've placed for participation in the band—or at least find a less powerful amplifier for the current rhythm guitarist. How do you respond?

1. How important is "quality" in a music ministry to you? How important is it to your students? Explain.
2. Would you allow a weaker musician to participate if he or she is faithful to all rehearsals? Why or why not?
3. Would you ever use a musical position as outreach to a student not already in a relationship with Christ? Why or why not?
4. Do you think supplementing a high school praise band with adult musicians undermines student ownership in the ministry? Why or why not?
5. What requirement regarding "spiritual maturity" do you have for musicians who lead worship? What is your rationale?
6. Is poor quality a reasonable price to pay as young musicians and worshipers are trained and gain experience in their craft? Why or why not?
7. Do you place more emphasis on high quality music when it comes to outreach events or events with larger percentages of adult participation? Why or why not?
8. G. K. Chesterton once said, "Anything truly worth doing is worth doing badly." What, if anything, does this have to say about musical praise and worship?

COMMUNION CREATIVITY

"Yeah, the last night of our missions trip to Mexico was really wonderful," reported a fellow youth worker. "We were all down on the beach praying and praising God, and then one of the students suggested we finish by taking communion. Now, we hadn't planned for that—but how often does one of your kids suggest a communion service? So we pooled our resources and came up with some potato chips and orange soda, and we had a service based on 1 Corinthians 11:23-30. It had a real feel of celebration because all week we'd been talking about Christ's resurrection, the absolute forgiveness of our sins, and our freedom and liberty in Jesus. Several students and adult leaders said it was a communion experience they'd never forget. But now I'm getting flack from a few older adults who thought what we did was inappropriate and disrespectful. I couldn't believe it! What do you think?"

1. How would you answer your youth ministry colleague?
2. What was your most memorable experience with communion?
3. What was your most creative experience with communion?
4. How creative are you willing to be in the use of elements for communion?
5. Some theological traditions only allow ordained clergy to administer communion. What are the advantages and disadvantages of this limitation? Explain your answer.
6. Some Christians believe a deeply introspective focus on self-reflection and confession is the only proper context for communion. What are the strengths and weaknesses of this singular approach? What other emotional contexts for communion do you feel are both biblical and appropriate?

IMPROVING YOUR BAPTISM

"Oh, no—we're having a baptism? I was really hoping the service would end on time today. A baptism always adds at least 15 minutes." You're a bit surprised to hear these words coming from one of your most faithful students. "I know it's important, and really exciting and meaningful for the person being baptized, but what about the rest of us? Half the time I don't even know the person, but we have to sit back and watch someone else's spiritual milestone. It's not like somebody else's baptism can have an impact on me."

1. What would you say to the student standing in front of you?
2. Theologian John Calvin wrote about "improving our baptism." What does this idea mean to you? Is observing others' baptisms an opportunity for believers to improve on their own baptisms? What other ideas come to your mind about how you might teach students to improve on their baptism?
3. What was the most meaningful baptismal service you have ever observed? What made it significant to you?
4. What can church leaders do to include other worshipers in the celebration of baptism?
5. Some ministries allow people who were most influential in the spiritual development of the person being baptized to participate in the baptismal service. What do you see as strengths and weaknesses of this practice?
6. Do you teach your students about the different Christian traditions regarding baptism? Why or why not?
7. What key biblical concepts can you name that are illustrated or celebrated in Christian baptism?

REBAPTISM?

The student sitting in front of you is speaking with a focused intensity: "Growing up my family attended church, but I didn't really understand much about Jesus until I got involved with a youth group in middle school. The summer after seventh grade, I attended a camp that was life changing for me. I made a serious commitment to live out my faith, and when the speaker asked if anyone wanted to be baptized, I raised my hand. It was a great service around the lake, my parents came up to camp for it, and all my friends were there. That next school year was great; I was involved in every aspect of the youth ministry and really grew spiritually. But the next year, when I got to high school, things began to change. I started dating a non-Christian, and it got pretty physical fast because we were sure we were in love. I started drinking and partying, especially when we broke up. I failed a couple of classes, skipped a lot of school, and became a discipline problem. My testimony around the school took a real beating. But this last month things began to turn around. I came across a bunch of pictures from the day I was baptized at summer camp and realized how much I was missing. I've repented and reestablished my friendships with my youth ministry friends. But I want a fresh start. So I'm wondering: Would you be willing to baptize me again to symbolize my renewed commitment to Christ?"

1. What would you say to the student sitting in front of you?
2. What are the potential advantages and disadvantages of baptizing students who have been baptized previously? What biblical and theological issues come into your consideration?
3. If you would be willing to rebaptize the student, what would you require of her? If not, is there some other form of public rededication or affirmation of baptism you would suggest?
4. Explain whether you would rebaptize a student in any of the following circumstances:

    a) If he/she were baptized as an infant, but wants to be baptized as a believer.

b) If he/she were baptized by sprinkling and wants to be immersed.
c) If he/she has fallen away from Christ and want to commemorate a fresh start.
d) If he/she were traveling in Israel and wants to be baptized in the Jordan River (as Jesus was).
e) Some other situation.

ARTS AND CREATIVITY

The feedback from your students was as clear as the pile of interest-and-assessment inventories neatly stacked on the corner of your desk. On the bright side, the students generally had great things to say about you, your staff, and the general direction of the program. It was clear that many of the youth were experiencing spiritual growth. But a number of students shared the same concern. Several mentioned that they had friends who were passionate about the arts yet left because they'd found that "there was nothing in the youth ministry for them." Even students who were actively involved expressed a desire for more opportunities to express their abilities in the visual arts, drama, music, dance, and general creativity. One student specifically mentioned the absence of painting, sculpture, drawing, and poetry in worship as his chief concern and the area of the ministry he felt most needed to grow. As you stand to stretch your legs and consider what the students are telling you, several questions pass through your mind.

1. What are some ways you could increase the use of the arts and creativity in your ministry?
2. In what ways do you incorporate the arts and other creative media into your worship times? How could you do more of this in the future?
3. What advantages do you see in emphasizing the arts more in your current ministry context? Do you see any potential disadvantages?

CHRISTMAS TRADITIONS

As you sip your cup of "holiday blend" coffee, your cell phone rings. It's one of your younger student leaders. As you wish her a jolly "Merry Christmas," she bursts in with an interruption. "I was just talking with a friend at school whose church doesn't celebrate Christmas with any of the stuff we take for granted. She said that Christmas trees, mistletoe, Yule logs, and holiday lights are all based on pagan practices that the church just adopted early on. So I have two questions: Are our Christmas traditions really based on pagan worship practices? And, if they are, why do we have a Christmas tree in our church?" As you stir a bit of cream into your coffee cup, you settle back to respond to her questions. What will you say?

WITH THIS RING . . .

"My fiancée and I would really like you to perform our wedding ceremony because of the impact you had on my life during high school. Even though she's never met you, she feels like she knows you because of the way I talk about you. And my parents think it's a great idea, too. We're getting married in Colorado, and that state doesn't have any specific requirements about who can perform a wedding. So we really hope you'll do it. Will you?"

1. What questions would you have for this couple to help you decide if you want to perform the service?
2. On a scale of 1 to 10, how comfortable would you be performing a wedding ceremony?
3. Do you have a set of standards that defines who you would or would not be willing to join in marriage? If so, what are they?
4. If you agree to perform the wedding, what premarital counseling would you offer, if any? Explain your answer.
5. How would you respond to someone who says, "If you don't do the wedding, they'll just find someone else who will—but you may end up alienating them from the church for good."

MAKING PRAYER "WORK"

The minute you pick up your cell phone, you can hear the sense of rising desperation in the voice on the other end. "Hi . . . uh, my name's David . . . We haven't met, but my best friend is part of your group. I'm calling because he says you know a lot about prayer. My grandmother has been diagnosed with cancer and the doctors say there's nothing else they can do. She needs a miracle. So I need you to tell me how to make prayer work. I've heard that God can do anything, and that Jesus healed people if they had enough faith. So how much faith do I need to get my prayer answered?" You take a deep breath while considering how you can communicate what you really believe about prayer in words this teenager will understand.

1. What spiritual issues can you identify from David's words?
2. Which of David's beliefs about how prayer works do you agree with? Which do you feel are mistaken or in need of correction?
3. What is your understanding of the relationship between a person's faith and answered prayer?
4. Do you see any danger in teaching methods to make prayer effective? If so, what are these dangers?
5. Have you ever experienced an answer to prayer that seemed miraculous? What lessons did that experience teach you about prayer and your relationship with God?
6. Have you ever prayed faithfully for something and not received it? What lessons, if any, did this teach you about prayer?
7. How would you explain to David that sometimes the most loving answer to prayer God can give is "no"?
8. How have your personal experiences with answered and unanswered prayer informed your views about God and intercession?

CONTEMPLATIVE PRAYER PRACTICES

You turn quickly when Jordan and Pat enter the youth room, knowing they'd spent the weekend with a church across town, attending its annual prayer retreat to support some friends who were providing student leadership for the event. "How was the retreat?" you ask. "Did your friends do a good job? Have your perspectives about prayer changed? Anything we can use to revitalize prayer in our own group?" The questions pour from your mouth with surprising speed.

"That's what we want to talk to you about," Jordan replies excitedly. "The retreat featured several ancient prayer practices, including walking a prayer labyrinth, praying the Scriptures, *lectio divina*, and the Jesus Prayer. We really liked some of them, but some of it felt so different that we didn't know what to think. What do you think about these kinds of prayer exercises?"

1. Which of the practices mentioned above have you experienced? Did you find them helpful?
2. Which of these practices have you used with students? How were they received?
3. What are your perceptions of the potential strengths and weaknesses of these practices?
4. What theological questions or concerns, if any, have you heard (or raised) regarding these practices? How do you respond to these questions?
5. On a scale of 1 to 10, how open are the adults who speak into your ministry to these practices?

PRAYING WITH YOUTH

"I just read a study that says that 72 percent of U.S. teenagers pray at least once a week.[20] And that's not just church kids—but all students. In light of that, don't you think we should spend more of our youth group time teaching about prayer—and actually praying?" You glance back at your intern who's been sharing and begin to reflect on the role of prayer within your ministry.

1. Do you think most youth ministry programs spend less time in prayer than they should? Why don't most programs pray more?
2. What percentage of your average youth meeting is spent in prayer?
3. On a scale of 1 to 10, how equipped are your students to pray aloud in a group setting? How equipped are they to pray in private? Explain your answer.
4. Describe the focus and results of the last teaching sessions you did on prayer.
5. Describe the most creative and engaging prayer experience you've ever led students through.
6. Would you recommend the Prayer of Jabez (1 Chronicles 4:9-10) as a model prayer for students? Explain your answer.
7. How many specific answers to your personal prayers could you articulate to students if you were asked?
8. Can praying certain themes be dangerous to a person's soul? After you answer look up Luke 18:9-14. Does this change your answer?
9. Are you concerned that teenage guys and girls praying together in pairs can lead to an inappropriate or unhealthy intimacy? Explain your answer.

---

20. http://www.barna.org/barna-update/article/16-teensnext-gen/93-what-teenagers-look-for-in-a-church

DOES PRAYER CHANGE GOD?

The questions were flying your way so fast that it was hard to stay focused on driving the van down the interstate. The informal setting seemed to have opened kids up, and they were tossing out questions that ranged from obscure biblical questions to inquiries about what you were like in high school. But you notice that Jeremy, one of your brightest students, hasn't said a word since the last rest stop. "What's on your mind, Jeremy?"

"Well, I've been thinking. If God has a plan for our lives, and a plan for the world, then what's the point of praying that something will happen? I mean, doesn't God already know what he's going to do? Do we really think we're gonna change God's mind?"

Suddenly, the van gets silent, as everyone waits to hear how you'll respond. What will you say?

DISTRACTED PRAYER

The question-and-answer time after your session on prayer was good. Kids were interested and engaged. But one question stayed in the forefront of your thinking even after the meeting concluded and you'd finished securing the building. Monica's question was very practical: "Whenever I set out to pray for any significant period of time, my mind soon wanders to what I need to do, how my day went, plans for the upcoming weekend, or whatever. Before I know it I'm no longer praying or even thinking about God. So how do *you* get back on track when distractions come to *your* mind?"

1. In what ways do you become distracted during prayer? How do you handle such distractions?
2. Do you think God ever speaks to us through the "distractions" we experience while praying? If so, how? Have you ever experienced this?
3. Do you ever write out your personal prayers? Why or why not?
4. What's the best advice you've ever received from a mentor regarding prayer?
5. What books or other resources have enriched your prayer life? Would you recommend these to students? Why or why not?
6. What biblical examples of prayer have most influenced you? Do you ever evaluate your prayers or the prayers of your students against these models? If not, why not?

HALFTIME EVANGELISM

"Come on—it will be great!" Alex, a friend from your local youth ministry network, is urging you to bring your students and their non-Christian friends to an evangelism event. "We are hooking a TV up to the big screens in the sanctuary to watch the biggest pro football game of the year. We're going to have sports-themed food and a 'rate the commercials' competition, and at halftime we're presenting the gospel using football illustrations and metaphors. The whole country is focused on football around the Super Bowl; we are just riding the excitement and momentum. After all, Jesus said we are to fish for people—we're just updating the bait."

1. Brainstorm the potential positives of a Super Bowl evangelism event.
2. Brainstorm possible negatives of such an event.
3. Would your ministry ever host an evangelism event built around the Super Bowl? Would you bring your students and their friends to such an event? Explain your answers.
4. How would you respond to someone who commented, "This sounds like a bait-and-switch—inviting people to come watch a football game and then slipping in some evangelism"?
5. Would you be comfortable using ministry funds to purchase NFL-licensed party goods to set the mood for such an evangelism event? Explain your answer.
6. How would you answer someone who raised a concern about linking the Prince of Peace with the violence of professional football?
7. Generally speaking, to what extent are you willing to build on popular cultural events as a way of gathering a crowd for an evangelism presentation?

THE MEDIUM AND THE MESSAGE

"Did you guys receive the invitation to the online seminar about Internet evangelism?" asks one of the youth workers at your monthly lunch gathering.

"I did," chimes in another youth pastor. "I'm psyched."

You didn't expect your fellow youth workers to be buzzing with excitement about evangelism and the Internet—but most of them are. "I think the seminar is connected to National Internet Evangelism Day," explains the first youth pastor. "People can receive training in all types of Internet evangelism from chat rooms, to Q & A on Christian Apologetics, to surveys, to 'Facebook evangelism,' to developing full-blown evangelistic websites. I think it's awesome."

"Well, I guess I'm not so sure," offers another youth pastor. "I know the Internet is the global marketplace of ideas, and it allows the gospel to reach places where it's often restricted. But I wonder about the long-term impact of any kind of gospel presentation that's divorced from personal interaction and relationships. And I also worry that the medium changes the gospel message in subtle ways that we don't even realize." Turning to you, she asks, "You've been pretty quiet. What do you think about Internet evangelism?"

1. Would you encourage your students to take part in an online training in Internet evangelism? Why or why not?
2. Do you agree or disagree with the idea that the medium changes the message?
3. What do you see as the strengths of Internet evangelism?
4. What do you see as the potential weaknesses of Internet evangelism?
5. What forms of ministry can be done effectively using the Internet?
6. What forms of ministry cannot be done on the Internet?

PREACHING WITHOUT WORDS

"Can you settle a disagreement we're having?" The request comes from two members of your student leadership team who are working on outreach ideas for next semester. "Pat says we can only use funds from our missions-and-evangelism budget if our planned activities include a verbal proclamation of the gospel. But I think specific, intentional acts of service can show the love of Christ in such a way that speaking the gospel is not always required—or even appropriate. After all," Jamie reiterates, "didn't Francis of Assisi say, 'Preach the gospel at all times. If necessary, use words'? I think some actions communicate Christ's message better than words."

1. What would you say in response to Pat and Jamie? What particular passages of Scripture would you suggest to help them understand your position?

2. How would you explain the connection between service and the verbal proclamation of the gospel?

3. Can you think of any service opportunity or ministry context that would preclude any verbal presentation of the gospel? Explain your answer.

4. If your students were planning an event where they were going to a city park on a hot day to hand out bottles of cold water, would you encourage them to say "Jesus loves you" each time they passed out a bottle? Would you encourage them to give out a Christian tract with each bottle of water? Why or why not?

5. Do people who contribute money to support the evangelistic efforts of your ministry expect a verbal or written gospel presentation to justify the use of their ministry gifts? How do you know?

CELEBRITY TESTIMONIES

"We've got a world-class skateboarder in our city who's now a Christian," Josh declared. "The guy won four medals at the last X Games. We should invite him to share his testimony at our yearly outreach event. Tons of kids will come just to meet him."

You'd heard about the skateboarder's recent conversion, but you've got a few questions: "How long has he been a Christian? Is he growing in faith and involved in a local faith community? Does he request a speaking fee? Does his testimony give a clear gospel presentation?"

Josh is short on answers but vehement in his opinion: "Everyone loves a celebrity—especially an athlete. People listen differently to celebrities than they listen to other people. I can't think of a better evangelism strategy!"

1. How would you respond to Josh's statement that people respond differently to celebrity testimonies?
2. What are the possible advantages of using a celebrity testimony as an evangelism tool? What possible disadvantages do you see?
3. What questions would you ask of a possible celebrity evangelist?
4. List five public figures whose personal testimonies would be of great interest to your students.
5. Suppose the celebrity Josh suggested was not an athlete but an actor—would this change your assessment? What if he were a musician? A politician? A military leader?
6. Would you ever invite a star athlete from a local high school to offer his or her evangelistic testimony at such an event? Under what circumstances?

EVANGELISM: PERSONAL OR PROGRAMMED?

Your ministry's student evangelism committee is at odds about how to spend the remainder of this year's evangelism budget. "We need to use the remaining funds on personal evangelism training," says Kelly. "We could send all our student leaders to a student training event or purchase a book on how to present the gospel and answer questions one-on-one with fellow students." Mark disagrees: "That's not a bad idea, but I think it'd be even better to host an evangelism event with lots of food and entertainment and a gifted comedian-evangelist who would provide an altar call. We could focus on training our student leaders to do follow-up and leave the gospel presentation to a professional." Both parties look to you for a decision on which plan to pursue.

1. Which plan would you choose based on your understanding of the students you work with? Explain the reasons for your answer.
2. List all the positive elements of stressing a personal, one-on-one evangelism.
3. List all the possible disadvantages of emphasizing a one-on-one evangelism strategy.
4. List the potential positives of "event evangelism."
5. List the possible negatives surrounding focusing your evangelism budget on a big event.
6. Do you believe the best evangelism strategy involves a mix of both event evangelism and personal evangelism—or are there other approaches that better match your philosophy of ministry? Explain your answer.

THE IRREDUCIBLE MINIMUM

"I think I just led my best friend to faith in Christ!" You smile as you hear the excited voice of one of your student leaders who's just called your cell phone. "It was just like you said. I simply started talking to Jamie about what Jesus was doing in my life, and before I knew it she said yes. So we said a prayer, and now she's accepted Christ."

"That's great!" you say, "but why did you begin by saying that you *think* you led Jamie to Christ?"

"Well, I never got to talk about sin or forgiveness or the cross or even heaven. I mostly talked about how Jesus is, like, always with me, and how with Jesus in my life I'm no longer feeling as alone as I go through my parents' divorce. So, I have to know: Did I tell her enough of the gospel to really lead Jamie to Christ?"

1. How would you respond to your student's question?
2. What essential truths must someone accept to be considered a Christian?
3. What biblical examples would you use to illustrate your concept of the basic gospel presentation?
4. Is it possible to separate the concept of Jesus as Savior from the concept of Jesus as Lord? Explain your answer.
5. How would you encourage your student to follow up with Jamie?

FIRE AND BRIMSTONE

"I just can't believe the evangelist who spoke to the youth at the church I visited last weekend," says one of your middle school students. "He did nothing but preach about hell: its flames, its eternal duration, even the 'wailing and gnashing of teeth.' I mean, who even talks like that? He acted like becoming a Christian was all just fire insurance and a way to eliminate eternal pain and suffering. Why would an adult present the gospel to a group of students like me where the focus is all on judgment? Do you think it's right to use all that talk about hell as a way of scaring kids into believing in Jesus?"

1. How would you explain your own beliefs about hell in a way a twelve-year-old could understand?
2. How frequently would you expect to mention hell in the next ten times you present the gospel to students? Explain your answer.
3. Can fear of hell be a legitimate and biblical motivation for a student (or any person) to enter into a relationship with Christ? Explain your answer.
4. How would you respond to someone who says, "The greatest backdrop for the shining grace of God is the darkness of an eternity in hell"?
5. Is the phrase "an eternity separated from God" synonymous with "suffering in hell forever"? Why or why not?

DOES THE "END" JUSTIFY THE MEANS?

"A soul is absolutely precious and beyond price. So even if one young person is saved, it is worth it." The speaker is an older member of your church who has just handed you a collection of "prophecy" DVDs that seem designed to scare unbelievers with vivid pictures of the end times. "When do you anticipate using them to help evangelize the students and visitors in the youth ministry?" he asks with a smile. How would you respond?

EQUIPPING STUDENTS TO FIND A CHURCH

When you walk into the meeting of your local youth ministry network, other youth workers are already discussing recent research about how to build in students a faith that will "stick."[21] One points out the troubling finding regarding the number of youth ministry kids who fail to connect with a local church or ministry after graduating from high school. Another laments: "Too many of our kids are 'graduating' from the faith when they graduate high school!" The hot topic seems to be how you can help students connect with a church after high school. Everyone seems to have a different list of criteria and priority items for helping kids find a church as well as the when and how to teach the subject. As you take a seat and order a large diet soda, all eyes turn to you.

1. What do you currently teach students in your ministry about the importance of connecting with a local church after they leave your ministry?
2. Do you engage in any particular activities to help students with this task (such as field trips, looking at church websites, etc.)? Why or why not?
3. What specific criteria do you present to students about selecting a church after graduation?
4. What else might you do to help build in students a faith that will last long beyond their time in your ministry?

---

21. For more on helping students build a faith that lasts, see Kara Powell, Brad Griffin, and Cheryl Crawford, *Sticky Faith, Youth Worker Edition: Practical Ideas to Nurture Long-Term Faith in Teenagers* (Grand Rapids: Zondervan, 2011).

PARTING WORDS

"So what do you plan to say to your graduating seniors at your last youth meeting of the year?" That's the first question your youth ministry colleague asks you as you sit down over an iced latte at the local coffee shop. You pause as you reflect on the privilege of having one more opportunity to speak to the seniors before they graduate from your ministry and head off to college, the military, or the job market. You've already given the question a lot of thought: What is it that these young men and women most need to hear from you as they head off into the next chapter of their lives? What will leave the most lasting impression on their minds? You have considered talking about prayer, community, spiritual gifts, gratitude, joy, wisdom, and a host of other topics, but you still haven't made a decision. Your friend continues, "Some youth ministry experts think that one of the most important things we youth workers can do is to help students know how to reestablish a relationship with Christ if they find that they've really 'blown it' or if they've set aside their identity as Christians for a time of exploration or 'fun' after high school. I'm thinking I might talk with my seniors about that. How about you?" You're both bothered and intrigued as you ponder your friend's statement and the possibilities for your final talk to graduating seniors.

1. If you were asked to give a final talk to graduates, what specific topic would you most want to speak with them about? Why?
2. How well equipped do you feel your students are to reconnect with Christ if they've experienced a major crisis of faith, moral failure, or temporary abandonment of their identity as Christians?
3. What can you do to help your students remember that God is always willing and eager to welcome them home, no matter what they've done?

GUIDELINES FOR WRITING YOUR OWN CASE STUDIES

Once you've become convinced of the profound impact case studies can have in training, developing, and refining youth workers, you may want to try your hand at writing your own. The following guidelines will help you become a competent writer of creative case studies in no time. Remember, these are just general guidelines; there may be times when you'll want to write case studies that go "outside the lines."

1. **Good case studies are short.** Let's be honest: Attention spans are not growing longer. So it stands to reason that it's easier to hold someone's attention for a short time rather than for a long time. I have sought to keep the case studies in this book relatively brief, focusing for the most part on a single scene. It is possible to explore more complex scenarios, but if that's your goal, consider doing so in progressive stages—allowing each stage to be a brief case study in and of itself. Make your studies long enough to introduce the essential facts but not so long that they become boring.

2. **Good case studies tell a story.** An interesting plot is essential to an impactful case study. When it comes to case studies, a solid plot requires an opening that will capture attention and a middle that supplies tension or refines the issues—all leading to a conclusion that does not yet exist, but will be supplied by the reader. An excellent study has a ring of authenticity and realism that allows the words to be translated into a mental picture. Provide enough detail and specifics to paint a relevant narrative that leads into open-ended discussion questions.

3. **Good case studies focus on a single issue.** For a case to really jump off the page and become a "living" thing that engages the reader, it must address a unique issue or situation of interest to the reader. Artificiality and vagueness are big problems in case study

development. Rather than exploring every possible facet of a huge topic, a good study investigates a specific and particular issue.

4. **Good case studies are set in the last 12 months.** The rapid changes in technology and other "essentials" of modern life (smart phones, Facebook, streaming video, etc.) mean that the context of youth ministry is ever-changing. In order to remain relevant, the best case studies are set in the context of the "now"—or at least within the last year. This allows for the exploration of seasonal issues, but keeps things current—which lends a sense of urgency and importance to the case study. While this does not mean one should never make use of an occasional "classical" or "historical" case, these must be used sparingly, if at all.

5. **Good case studies include the voices of realistic characters.** There's simply no better way to help the reader connect with a case study than through allowing the character or characters to speak. Most elements of life, drama, and personality are best communicated through dialogue. In addition to spoken dialogue, quotations from letters, text messages, emails, and songs can also be used effectively.

6. **Good case studies are designed to aid ministry development.** Two important questions should be asked when developing a case study: First, what function will this case study play in the ministry development of the user? Second, what elements and details can be included to promote thinking in new areas of ministry that may not have been explored yet? If you are clear on the relevance of the study to the real needs of youth ministry, that focus will be reflected in the development of the case study. Often, studies can be written with a deliberate ambiguity that enables the case to be equally applicable for youth workers in both church and parachurch contexts.

7. **Good case studies employ empathetic characters.** A key element of empathy is connection. One surefire way to build this connection is to link the experience and needs of the characters in the study to the real and felt needs of the reader. The most impactful case studies are those in which the users feel they share common values and experiences with the characters in the study. Revela-

tions about a character's attributes or emotions will often influence how decisions are made and how questions are answered.

8. **Good case studies welcome disagreement and multiple perspectives.** Many of the best case studies feature issues or situations about which reasonable, knowledgeable, and godly people may disagree. This possibility of conflict forces deeper reflection and can promote learning on several different levels. Regardless of one's particular views on a controversial issue, it behooves both writers and users of a study to treat all perspectives fairly and respectfully. The goal is to encourage each user to work through the issue personally and develop at least a preliminary strategy for engaging the situation. This forced decision-making is consistent with educational dissidence so popular with educators due to its deep, life-changing impact.

9. **Good case studies are general enough to be relevant to multiple contexts.** When possible, avoid writing studies that are significant only within a particular denomination, location, age group, theological leaning, ministry context, or racial/ethnic group. The best studies are germane to potential users in a wide range of contexts. Truly exceptional case studies have the ability to be used by ministry novices as well as long-term professionals. Generalities allow multiple groups to wrestle with the central issue within their own depth of ministry experience and skill level. Many good case studies go so far as to use gender-neutral names like Pat, Shawn, Chris, or Jamie to avoid reinforcing gender stereotypes.

10. **Good case studies include carefully designed questions.** When writing case studies, I often begin with a question that invites an open-ended response to the central situation being presented. This first question often serves as the conclusion to the narrative portion of the case story and helps to set the stage for more specific and detailed questions that follow. A few well-written questions are much more effective than a long list of unrefined questions. (If nothing else, the issue of time comes into play when there are too many questions.) Take care to utilize different types and styles of questions.

Share Your Thoughts

With the Author: Your comments will be forwarded to the author when you send them to *zauthor@zondervan.com*.

With Zondervan: Submit your review of this book by writing to *zreview@zondervan.com*.

Free Online Resources at
www.zondervan.com

Zondervan AuthorTracker: Be notified whenever your favorite authors publish new books, go on tour, or post an update about what's happening in their lives at www.zondervan.com/authortracker.

Daily Bible Verses and Devotions: Enrich your life with daily Bible verses or devotions that help you start every morning focused on God. Visit www.zondervan.com/newsletters.

Free Email Publications: Sign up for newsletters on Christian living, academic resources, church ministry, fiction, children's resources, and more. Visit www.zondervan.com/newsletters.

Zondervan Bible Search: Find and compare Bible passages in a variety of translations at www.zondervanbiblesearch.com.

Other Benefits: Register yourself to receive online benefits like coupons and special offers, or to participate in research.

ZONDERVAN

ZONDERVAN.com/
AUTHORTRACKER
follow your favorite authors